GROWING

UP

BORDERLINE

A Mother's Memoir

GROWING UP BORDERLINE

A Mother's Memoir

Linda Burch

BALLEO PUBLISHING, New York

...

This is a true story, told exactly as it occurred to the best of my memory. The names of people and places have been changed to protect privacy.

ISBN 978-0989709507

Library of Congress Control Number: 2013915497

Burch, Linda

Non-fiction

www.GrowingUpBorderline.com

Printed in the United States of America

First Edition

Dedication

To my incredible husband, Bill, my rock and my soul mate.
His love is a gift I open every day;

to my tolerant, loving, and patient son, Brian;

and, of course,

to my daughter, Lisa, with whom there is never a dull moment and who allowed me tell her story so that it might help others.

A child needs your love most when he deserves
it least.

                              --Erma Bombeck

Contents

FOREWORD

People ask me, "When did you know there was something wrong with your child?" My glib response is usually, "When she never grew out of her 'terrible twos.'" The truth is, however, that I suspected a problem even before that. Unfortunately, no one in the medical or mental health professions could tell me what it was, much less what to do about it. Everyone in my family struggled for years, feeling helpless and just wanting the problem to go away.

When my daughter was finally diagnosed with borderline personality disorder at the age of eighteen, I felt a convolution of relief, anxiety, and anger: relief because we finally had a diagnosis—a name for her problem, anxiety because there was virtually no treatment available at that time, and anger because medical professionals had refused to diagnose it earlier. The havoc within our family system had already occurred.

This book is a memoir, not a manual. My goal is not to tell you what to do, but rather, what I did. As a parent I did many things wrong. Would I have done them differently with an earlier, accurate diagnosis? Yes, many of them, but which ones and how? You decide.

I hope this book can give parents and teachers an understanding of the importance of early recognition of children and teens with symptoms of mental illness and the urgency of early intervention on their behalf. If you are a family member or friend of someone with mental illness, you may recognize and identify with some of my experiences. Above all, I hope you will take comfort in hearing my story and knowing you are not alone.

--Linda Burch

Chapter 1

Somewhere in the Middle of the Story

Six Meadows Treatment Center
October 22, 1997

Dear Mom,

Hi, how are you? I could be a lot better. I had a really bad morning. I went haywire just like I used to do in Mr. B's class. I hate it here. I'm not doing so hot. I just feel like giving up and I don't know what to do. Please get me out of here. I can't stand it any longer. I used to like this place but now I hate it. I'm scared to death of my roommate. She said she was going to beat me.

Please, mommy, come and take your baby back home. I promise I won't do anything stupid. I want to be given a second chance. Let me prove to you that I don't need to be locked up. I am counting on you. Well, gotta go.

Love, Lisa

Chapter 2

Blissful Beginnings

I had never felt this happy. I was rocking my ten-day-old daughter, Lisa, while my three-and-a-half-year-old son, Brian, was playing with his trucks at my feet. It had been a seemingly endless, three-year grueling process to adopt our two children, and now they were both ours. I had everything I ever wanted right there in the room with me.

My husband David and I had been married eight years, and when we were told that we could never have children biologically, it was as if my world had ended. Now I had my dream back, and I felt my life had been given great purpose. I fantasized about watching them grow and develop, and I was so thankful to have been given this great gift.

Brian's early years had been marked with numerous ear infections and trips to the pediatrician, but Lisa was remarkably physically healthy. She presented other types of challenges, however. It was extremely difficult to get her to sleep as a baby, and when she awoke during the night, she was inconsolable.

By the age of four months, she was very "high energy" and constantly in motion. When she became tired, she moved around even more. I would see her start to drift off, only to have her jerk herself awake, wave her arms and look around as if she were missing something. She would bring her knees up to her chest, straighten her legs, and then slam her heels down on the bed. Every sleep time was a huge ordeal, and it often took hours to get her to sleep.

She was not a snuggler and did not like to be confined, so holding her or rocking or walking was never effective. Feeding helped only for awhile, and she never took a pacifier.

We were told by our pediatrician that we should just let her cry until she tires herself out, but that was really difficult for me to do. I know all mothers hate to hear their children cry, but as an adoptive mother, I was so grateful finally to be a parent that I was really reluctant to let my child "suffer" in any way. I didn't want her to feel abandoned by yet another mother.

Nonetheless, I did what the pediatrician suggested. I went into her room to assure that she was dry and that nothing was "poking" her, reassured and comforted her for a moment, and then went back to bed to lie awake listening to her howl for hours. All I knew was that my sleepless, agitated child wasn't acting right.

When she was a few months older and teething, my husband would rock her on the big lounge chair and rub her gums with whiskey. He joked that every time he would rub her gums with a finger dipped in whiskey, he took a "slug" from the bottle himself. When I woke up in the morning and went to check on them, I would find both of them sound asleep in the chair.

Chapter 3

Terrible Twos

My daughter wouldn't sit still, even for meals, and nothing seemed to make her happy. She possessed two states of being: screaming or not screaming.

Once, we were eating dinner at a nice seafood restaurant in Galveston with some out-of-town friends, and the food was taking a long time to be served. Lisa had already eaten her dinner and all her snacks, and she was bored with the toys we brought along, so she began screaming at the top of her lungs.

Nothing any of us could do would distract her or quiet her. As our food finally arrived, my husband decided he just had to take her outside. As he carried her through the restaurant, two or three people sitting at another table actually began clapping. Soon half the restaurant was applauding as David and Lisa walked out of the restaurant.

I was humiliated and wanted to crawl under the table, but my friend was livid with anger toward the applauding patrons. She turned to the next table and admonished, "You people are so rude! Haven't you had children yourselves?"

I ate my food in a couple of gulps and then went outside to take over caring for Lisa so David could return to the restaurant and finish his dinner. Exploding with energy, she was running around the parking lot.

The terrible twos seemed to drag into her third and fourth years. I enrolled her in a mother's-day-out program at a local church. Because Lisa could be very charming at times, her teachers generally liked her, although they reported she had difficulty sitting still, following directions, and controlling her impulses. She had a high level of energy and moved constantly, including running wildly around the playground.

One teacher remarked that she thought Lisa would be an art teacher when she grew up. I was a bit surprised, so I asked why she felt that way. The teacher replied, "Because she finishes her own project and then goes around the room helping everyone else with theirs."

It was a kind way to say Lisa couldn't sit still.

When we went to the grocery store, she refused to sit in the shopping cart. However, when I allowed her to walk beside me, she would take items from the shelves and open them, or she would throw tantrums if I didn't buy her what she wanted.

One day her drama was unleashed on unsuspecting shoppers when she decided she wanted a bag of Gummi Bears. We were in the checkout line when she grabbed the bag off the shelf and announced that she had to have them.

"No Gummi Bears. They will rot your teeth," I responded. "Put them back."

Lisa threw herself on the floor and screamed like a person who perhaps had just found out that her pet, her best friend, and her family had all died at once. She continued to scream at about seven million decibels, "I WANT THEM, I WANT THEM," over and over.

My discomfort was mounting as I noticed other shoppers were actually stopping by our checkout line to stare—at me. They weren't being disapproving of Lisa; they were being disapproving of me. I couldn't get out of there fast enough.

Once when David took her to the grocery store with him, he lifted her up and, despite her screaming objections, placed her into the children's seat of the shopping cart. She began bouncing around in the cart so violently that he quickly, angrily, and roughly lifted her out of the basket.

At the same time, two ladies, one in her thirties and the other in her late sixties, approached them. The younger one, fearing that my husband was about to spank Lisa, exclaimed, "Don't you dare hit that child!"

Almost at the very same time, the older lady admonished, "That child needs a good spanking!" Then the two women started arguing with one another about how my husband should handle Lisa.

My husband was too frustrated to find any humor in the situation, so he grabbed Lisa by the hand and quickly moved to the next aisle, leaving the two women to discuss child rearing practices.

Chapter 4

Where Is My Hot Dog?

One evening after dinner I took Lisa across the street to the playground at the church where she attended the mother's-day-out program. After playing on the swing and slide, we had a quiet moment as we sat together on a two-person glider.

She looked up at me, and in a wistful voice asked, "Mommy, why did you and Daddy cut off my hot dog?"

I was dumbfounded. When I regained my composure, I asked, "What do you mean, Sweetheart?"

"Well, Brian never gets into any trouble, and I am always in trouble. He has a hot dog, and I don't, so I figured you cut it off when you adopted me. I just want to know why."

This was one child-rearing issue that I hadn't read about in the books, so I had to scramble to come up with an explanation appropriate for a four-year-old about how boys and girls were different. What bothered me, though, was that she had blamed me for her difference.

Lisa had to be watched at all times. It took her only seconds to get into real trouble with possible serious consequences.One day at my parents' farm, the entire family went fishing in one of the stock ponds. Everyone had a hook in the water except Lisa, who was playing in the dirt nearby. I was watching my fishing line with frequent glances toward Lisa. On one of those glances, I couldn't believe what I was seeing.

Lisa was walking toward the water, but as she got to the edge of the water, she didn't stop—she continued into the water. As if in a trance or a daze or as if she were sleepwalking, she walked directly toward the center of the pond and didn't stop until her head was below the surface of the turbid water.

I screamed her name and jumped into the water after her. By this time she was totally submerged and I couldn't see her anymore, but I kept focused on the spot near the center of the pond where her head had disappeared under the dark and gloomy water. I waded out to that spot, and with the water up to my chest, I began frantically feeling around in the murky water, trying to locate her.

After a few seconds that felt like an eternity, I felt her head, which was about two feet below the water. Grabbing her by the hair, I pulled her head above the water and held her close to me. Unfortunately, the combined weight of both of us caused me to sink deep into the sandy bottom of the pond. I was stuck and couldn't move.

By now David had waded partway into the water with his fishing pole and held it out toward me. Holding on to Lisa with one arm, I grabbed the pole with the other, and David pulled both of us out.

My entire body was trembling as I realized that if I had waited just seconds more to glance in her direction, she would have disappeared without anyone knowing that she was in the middle of the pond. It was a bizarre experience that shook me to my bones.

Chapter 5

To Start or Not to Start

Lisa had the rare fortune of have a magical birthday of September first. It was special because in the state of Texas, September first is the official date by which a child must have turned five before he or she can begin public kindergarten. A child who turns five after September first must wait for another year to start school.

What did that mean for Lisa, whose birthday was exactly on September first? The answer was that we had a choice. We could start her in public school in either of the two years—the year she turned five (and be the youngest in her class) or the year she turned six (and be the oldest in her class).

Many factors entered into our decision, including her maturity, her size, the fact that she was a girl (and girls often are more advanced than boys at that age), and her achievement in mother's-day-out and pre-school. After much stress and debate, we decided to go ahead and let her begin the earlier of the two possible years for one overwhelming reason: if it didn't work out because she was not ready, she could simply repeat kindergarten and still be within normal parameters of age and grade. Oh yes, and there was one other reason. There was no doubt that there was one person who was ready for her to start school-

9

-me. I was ready to have her in class for the full day, not just a few hours a day in pre-school.

The first day of kindergarten was exciting for all of us. I knew we were embarking on a grand adventure which would present us with challenges we couldn't even imagine at that point. With mixed feelings of joy and anxiety, I accompanied her, looking like a tourist with camera in hand, to the school and met her teacher, Mrs. Black.

Mrs. Black was a middle-aged, slim lady with many years of experience and a warm smile that assured me everything was going to be fine.

Everything WAS fine, for the most part. Lisa's kindergarten report cards showed mastery of reading, listening, speaking, language, handwriting, art, music, physical education, health, math, social studies, science, and fine motor skills. In addition, it was noted that she had good work habits, including taking care of materials and working neatly. She received a "satisfactory" in conduct in every one of the six grading periods.

At the end of the year, I conferred with Mrs. Black to determine whether or not Lisa should be held back, given the circumstances of her September first birthday. Mrs. Black unequivocally said that Lisa should definitely go on to first grade. *Yes!*

I was very hopeful after her successful kindergarten experience, and both Lisa and I eagerly awaited the new school term and first grade.

While out of school during the summer, though, she constantly presented challenges with her behavior at home and out in public. She refused to go to sleep at night, often ran around screaming, threw tantrums, was always fidgety, interrupted people, and argued with and pestered her big brother endlessly. She was always on the go and was rarely able to play quietly. When she was hungry, she didn't just become irritable, like most kids. She would completely fall apart.

We couldn't take her to church with us because she couldn't sit through a Mass without a meltdown, which embarrassed us, especially when we would from other people get glares which said, "Can't you control your child?" Her dad and I went to separate services so that one of us could be at home with her.

David and I tried to exert more control over Lisa, but there was no improvement in her interruptions, blurted remarks, and violation of rules. In fact, the tougher we were, the worse she got. *Was she inherently bad or just a kid being a kid? Or was she being willfully and intentionally disruptive because of how we were rearing her?*

My parents were constantly asking me, "Why don't you do something about that kid?" Other adults counseled us not to worry. "Just hang in there," they advised, "and by adolescence Lisa will have outgrown it."

It was heart-breaking and nerve-wracking.

The day finally came for school to start. We met her first-grade teacher, Miss Schulz, on the first day, and I was immediately struck by the contrast between her and Mrs. Black. Miss Schulz was quite young and was clearly only recently out of college. She was a direct contrast to the experienced, calm, motherly Mrs. Black, and I was concerned from the moment I met her that Lisa's first grade experience would be more difficult than her kindergarten time. I pushed my concerns to the back of my mind and hoped for the best.

The students received no report cards the first six-week reporting period, but everything seemed to be going okay. The second reporting period, Lisa received an "excellent" or "satisfactory" in every category. She even received an "excellent" in conduct and a note from Miss Schulz saying, "I enjoy having Lisa in my class!"

After Christmas, things began going downhill. After the first day of school after the holiday break, Lisa brought home a progress report, which stated, "The student is presently in academic difficulty in this grade, and consequently there is the danger of failure. The causes on the form that were checked were "lack of serious approach to studies" and "lack of attention in class."

What was interesting, though, were the boxes that were NOT checked: poor attention, failing grades, and inadequate preparation. Consequently, we assumed her performance had been acceptable in those areas.

The boxes that were checked for the teacher's recommendations were "more effort" and "complete work assignments." Again, there were several boxes left unchecked: turn homework in on time, attend tutorials, and confer with teacher.

Lisa's dad, David, and I had a talk with her about her poor conduct grade and the progress report, but we really weren't too upset because she still seemed to be doing well in her academic subjects. Since the box marked "conference with teacher" was not marked, we decided to wait and see how the next grading period went, which would also be the end of the first semester.

The report card arrived at the end of January. Lisa's reading grade had only fallen two points, from 84 to 82, but her conduct grade was an N, which mean "needs improvement." Her language grade fell from 87 to 66, and her math grade fell from 93 to 77. Nonetheless, her overall average for the fall semester showed she was still passing all subjects.

Soon after the spring semester began at the end of January, David and I were called in for a number of conferences. Miss Schulz reported to us that Lisa's behavior in class was disorganized and impulsive. She was unable to work independently, unable to sustain attention, and unable to complete assignments. Her out-of-seat behavior was a disruption to the other students.

Clearly, Miss Schulz was overwhelmed. As David esoterically put it, "Lisa had her treed like a dog trees a raccoon." I told her that Mrs. Black had not mentioned any of those behaviors during kindergarten and gently suggested to Miss Schulz that she speak to Mrs. Black about Lisa and the approaches Mrs. Black used. Miss Schulz coldly responded that this was now first grade, which required much more discipline than kindergarten had. In other words, she was refusing to ask for suggestions or advice from a much more experienced teacher. Also, I probably insulted her by suggesting Mrs. Black could handle Lisa and she couldn't.

The behavioral problems at school and at home continued and progressed during the next two months. However, during the fourth six-week reporting period, she brought up her grades in almost every subject: 88 in reading, 85 in language arts, 73 in math, and a 92 in each of two new subjects introduced at the beginning of the semester: social studies and science. But there was that pesky N in conduct again.

Chapter 6

What's Wrong with My Child?

We began working with a therapist, Dr. Gunnery, to improve Lisa's behavior at home and at school. The doctor recommended two types of evaluations: visual and psychological. Thus began many years of innumerable tests to try to determine what Lisa's problems were and what was causing them.

The first step was to evaluate her vision skills to determine if she had any problems recognizing and interpreting information taken in through sight. The vision skills we need to understand, analyze, and interpret what we see are called visual perception. A problem with visual perception is one of the most common causes of learning disabilities because so much information in the classroom is presented visually. This involves testing not only the sharpness of vision but also how the brain processes what the eye sees.

The results showed that for a child of six, she was "marginally developed" in perception skills. This was not enough to warrant special accommodations in the school, so the ophthalmologist recommended a developmental program of workbooks and other activity sheets for us to do at home to develop skills.One of the skills we worked on was visual memory, or remembering what she saw in a picture, and something called "figure ground," which is the skill that lets us pick out details without getting confused by the background or surrounding images. This skill is especially helpful when we are presented with a lot of visual information at one time. Finding "hidden pictures" within images was a good exercise for this.

The doctor warned us that Lisa was at risk for "falling through the cracks" of the educational system because her perception problems were not severe enough to qualify for special accommodations, but they were bad enough to cause a lot of difficulty in her classes for the rest of her life if they weren't addressed. We would be cautioned with this "falling through the cracks" metaphor many more times by many more professionals.

The next step in our quest to determine how to improve Lisa's behavior was the psycho-educational evaluation by a highly-regarded child psychiatrist, Dr. Merle. This test would determine whether Lisa's difficulties were caused by the fact that she is young for her grade placement, by a learning disability, or by a possible combination of the two. Dr. Merle began her evaluation by interviewing Lisa's dad and me. We summarized her behaviors this way:

"Lisa has been strong-willed and demanding at home since birth, yet she is well-behaved with sitters and with her grandmother. She had some behavior and discipline problems in preschool and mother's-day-out at the age of four, but in kindergarten she did well, and her behavior was adequate. We attribute this success to her teacher who established and consistently upheld limits, boundaries, and expectations. This year she began to encounter behavioral and academic difficulties. We would describe her as an immature youngster who wants help with things she should do alone, wants to run things, fails to finish what she starts, is restless and overactive, tells stories which did not happen, and has demands which must be met immediately. We want to see her improve her behavior and academic performances."

Dr. Merle then gave Lisa a comprehensive battery of eleven different tests in three separate sessions before meeting with us in March with her conclusions. Her bottom-line assessment was that Lisa was not ready for first grade.

She believed that Lisa felt unsuccessful because she could not do the things that first graders are expected to do, so she was defiant and had become emotionally needy, saying "I don't want to" when she couldn't. Her IQ tested as low average, and she had a low amount of general knowledge information. She was not picking up information on her own, she had to be told repeatedly, and she had significant attention and emotional difficulties. The "story-telling" tests revealed emotional disturbance, as Lisa had related stories about abused dogs, throwing up, and death.

Unfortunately, Dr. Merle could not pinpoint a diagnosis or reason behind Lisa's difficulties. She said they could stem from an attention deficit, from a brain processing disorder, or from a language processing irregularity. *What? I could only hear the words, but I didn't know what they meant.*

Dr. Merle recommended that we "write off" the first grade and repeat it next year in a private school, if necessary. She also recommended speech therapy, an assessment of Lisa's language functioning, and continued psychological therapy with Dr. Gunnery. She also wanted to repeat her battery of tests in one year.

Well, this was not exactly what we wanted to hear. We were left with no choice but to withdraw her from public school, which we did at the end of March, and place her in an alternate, private school. The only private school in our area that had openings this late in the year was the Montessori School.

What a mistake that was! After only a few weeks, we were told by staff and teachers that a Montessori is not an appropriate placement for someone with Lisa's issues. To be successful in a

Montessori, a child has to be a self-starter and an independent learner, neither of which Lisa was.

We spent the summer in speech therapy and psychological counseling with Dr. Gunnery. Lisa enjoyed the one-on-one attention she received during these visits and eagerly awaited each session.

When the new school term began in September, at the recommendation of Dr. Gunnery, we enrolled Lisa in the partial hospitalization program (PHP) or "day school" of Baymont Hospital, a nearby psychiatric facility. The program provides treatment for emotionally disturbed and behaviorally challenged children through group activities, occupational therapy, and individual and family therapy. At the same time, she received academic instruction in a highly structured environment with a low student-teacher ratio. She was diagnosed with attention deficit hyperactivity disorder and placed on Ritalin, with dosage monitored closely by a psychiatrist.

We were counseled that ADHD is often mistakenly blamed on parenting, but research shows ADHD is a medical disorder, characterized by differences in brain structure and function.

It was a relief to know that we weren't bad parents, but we were cautioned that children with ADHD require more time, attention, and structure from their parents than children without ADHD. They generally don't understand rules and may test parents' limits repeatedly. The entire family constantly has to cope with the troubles the child is having at home, in school, and socially. Often other children in the family may feel neglected because their ADHD sibling requires so much attention.

Finally, we were warned, research shows that dealing with a child who had ADHD often causes frustration, personal stress, and severe marital strain for parents. *That was us, all right.*

Chapter 7

To Ritalin or Not to Ritalin

During this time—the late 1980's—the use of Ritalin was being questioned, as was the perceived over-diagnosis of ADHD, attention deficit hyperactivity disorder. There was a growing negative image of Ritalin and other medications that doctors believed helped children function socially and academically. Almost a million children were taking the drug, which resulted in a growing belief on the part of some of the public that doctors were too eager to diagnose a child as having ADHD. Critics were calling it the "fashionable diagnosis" that classified children as mentally abnormal, a negative moniker that would follow them through their school years.

The controversy was unimportant to me because all I cared about was whether or not my child could see a benefit. If Ritalin made it possible to help her learn, then it was well worth trying in spite of any controversy over the diagnosis of ADHD or over the use of stimulant medication.

As it turned out, Lisa's academic progress while at Baymont and while receiving Ritalin was phenomenal. Although officially repeating first grade, she was reading at a fourth grade level. She was having less problematic impulsive behavior both at home and at school. She had an increased ability to stick with writing projects until they were completed and had more appropriate social interactions, such as listening, not interrupting, sharing, etc.

Because of the controversy over Ritalin's possible negative effects, including studies that suggested Ritalin stunts the growth of children when taken three times a day every day, I tried to keep Lisa off the medication during weekends and evenings. I could see a marked increase in her hyperactive symptoms during those times, so I always joked that I only gave her a Ritalin when **I** needed it.

We were fortunate to have excellent medical and mental health insurance through the company Lisa's dad worked for as a chemical engineer. The Baymont School charged $85 per day, plus $130 every time the psychiatrist or social worker saw her one-on-one. This amounted to about $3,500 per month, of which insurance paid 80%.

To receive this reimbursement, however, the doctor had to play games with her diagnosis. Since ADHD did not fall under our plan as a mental health need, her diagnosis officially became oppositional defiant disorder (ODD), which was covered. However, studies have shown that about half of children who have ADHD also have ODD, which manifests in socially unacceptable behaviors, so it wasn't much of a stretch to consider ODD as a diagnosis at this point. Treatment didn't change because the recommended medication for both disorders was Ritalin.

Playing the insurance game was something we would learn to do well in the coming years. It wasn't easy, but I familiarized myself with our particular plan so that I could become an active advocate for my child within its guidelines. I needed to know if I needed a referral for counselors, therapists and child psychiatrists; what services the plan covered; how many visits were covered; if certain diagnoses were excluded; which treatments were deemed unnecessary for certain diagnoses; etc. I quickly discovered that mental health coverage was far inferior to medical-surgical coverage, so it became even more important to study our plan. I knew that understanding our insurance benefits could save thousands of dollars in unexpected out-of-pocket expenses.

Health insurance coverage continues to be a source of much stress and inequity for people with mental illness in America. Health insurance is a lifeline for many people with mental illness, as expensive medications and numerous doctors' visits are commonly needed to manage their illness. However, many people who have insurance often find that their mental health benefits restrict access to necessary care or denies claims for a variety of reasons.

I don't know how people get help for mental illness if they have no insurance and the effect of their illness is making them lack the need to continue living or the desire to find a job that offers insurance.

Chapter 8

Bloody Head

During Lisa's "partial hospitalization" and second attempt at first grade, one of her therapists told me about a seminar being conducted by a local Ph.D., Steven Goldman, who specialized in treating children with ADHD. His treatment theory was based on the premise that ADHD children cannot manage the insides of their brains. Some of the examples he gave described Lisa perfectly.

Dr. Goldman said that ADHD children often have a time disorder. For most of us, "next week" or "next month" has a relevance to us that we can relate to and understand. This concept is unreal to ADHDs. This was certainly true of Lisa. She was not able to construct an image mentally that enabled her to grasp the idea of time. To her, one hour had the same meaning as one year.

Another example was the ubiquitous parental phrase "Be good!" The ADHD child has no idea what "good" means. He or she is unable to cognitively process many terms and concepts internally. In Lisa's case, she couldn't process the danger of running out into the street despite being warned of "being hit by a car." It wasn't until a babysitter put it into a graphic word picture Lisa could understand that she stopped her reckless behavior.

21

The babysitter told her that she would get a bloody head if she ran into the street. "Bloody head" was an impression she could process and comprehend mentally.

Everything Dr. Goldman said made a lot of sense and described her perfectly. I was relieved to discover that his comprehensive approach of both psychological and medical treatment was one that we were already following. He also stressed the importance of adapting parenting techniques and strategies to children with ADHD.

With Lisa, myriads of everyday tasks turned into battles all day—from getting her out of bed in the morning to getting her to bed at night. Everything was a tug of war. I read every book I could find, but none of the parenting tips worked, including the universal behavior modification tool of "timeout."

I could never get Lisa to respond to timeouts. First of all, it was nearly impossible to get her into the timeout space. She would always refuse to go, resulting in my having to physically drag her to the area, just to be followed by her running away. I tried locking her door, and she responded by breaking it down. After we reinforced the door, she began to bang her head on the wall until there were holes in the wall and lumps on her head.

It was a relief when Dr. Goldman told us that the popular intervention of timeout rarely works in the presence of ADHD. However, he had no magic cure to replace it except to use positive attention instead of punishment to stimulate the child's development. In other words, move away from punishment and move toward rewarded behavior. *I had to re-train myself and my parenting strategy. Timeouts worked great for Brian, but now I had to use a different method for Lisa.*

As a parent, it was my instinct to jump on irritating behaviors and try to correct them, simply to make them go away. According to Dr. Goldman, this was rewarding the inappropriate behavior because with ADHD children any kind of attention is better than no attention at all. He suggested rewarding a child with praise, good works, smiles, and pats on the back as often as we can.

Do I have to tell you that this didn't work? Of course, we didn't know then that the ADHD diagnosis was just the tip of the iceberg.

The one-year follow-up psychological tests to determine her emotional functioning took place at the end of her first grade year at Baymont Day School. Dr. Merle, who had done the testing the prior year, administered the battery of nine tests over two days.

The results, some of which were consistent with previous testing and others which identified new and unusual problems, puzzled the professionals. Lisa did not seem to fit any category or any "neat" description. Again, we heard the term "falling through the cracks" because her problems couldn't be pigeon-holed into a diagnosis that had a name.

No one realized then that what she was exhibiting would soon be identified in the psychiatric world as traits of borderline personality disorder: "limited common sense and social judgment; defensive when faced with intense emotions; emotionally needy; misreads social situations; poor coping strategies."

Lisa returned to the public elementary school the next year, where she completed her second and third grades with carefully-selected, nurturing teachers whose limits, expectations, and consequences were firmly established and maintained. It wasn't smooth sailing, but we got through both grades with the help of frequent teacher conferences.

During the second grade, however, she developed a condition known as trichotillomania, or hair pulling disorder. Trichotillomania is a mental impulse-control disorder that involves an irresistible urge to pull out hair.

For Lisa, the behavior escalated to the point of very noticeable hair loss. She pulled out not only her scalp hair, but also all of her eyelashes and eyebrow hair. Sometimes she was not fully consciously aware that she was pulling her hair. She seemed to go into a trance; other times, she reported an increasing sense of tension and a great need to pull out her hair because of the relief when doing so.

Because she was fair-skinned and red-haired, the absence of lashes and brows was not obvious at a distance, but it nonetheless changed her appearance dramatically. Her psychiatrist placed her on the medication Anafranil for anxiety, which helped calm the impulses. However, it took over a year for her hair, brows, and lashes to grow back.

Chapter 9

Pigs and Turtles and Seeing Eye Dogs

Each spring of her second and third grades, I signed Lisa up for the local Girls' Softball League. I love baseball, and since I had enjoyed being an assistant coach of Brian's youth baseball team for several years, I wanted to do the same with Lisa. So, in order to monitor her behavior and keep an eye on her, I happily volunteered as assistant coach and team mom.

Lisa got along well with the other girls and was known as the clown on the team. She was skinny as a rail and very fast, so if she ever got on base, she came all the way home to score on any kind of hit. Getting on base was the problem, though, because she couldn't hit the ball, so she used the "don't swing and wait for a walk" strategy. A walk was a sure score for her. If she was on first and the next batter hit the ball, she just kept running from second to third to home, as the fielders threw from one base to the other in vain.

In girls' softball, the best players are usually the pitcher and infielders, except for the third baseman, who is there simply to mark the base. Outfield was another position for girls who weren't particularly blessed in athletic prowess. They would stand around the outfield, chatting with one another, watching airplanes, picking at their fingernails, thinking about Barbie dolls, etc. It really didn't matter because they couldn't catch a fly ball anyway.

If a ball was hit into the outfield, the parent of that fielder would yell excitedly in an effort to notify their child that the ball is headed her way. Otherwise, she'd probably never notice it. Startled, the child would look around frantically until she located the ball, picked it up, and hurled it in a random direction.

This caused some other parent to try to activate his or her child, and the ball would be hurled again and again until the runner eventually chugged in for a score. Even if the ball made it to the catcher before the runner stepped on the plate for a home-run, chances were good that the catcher, wearing a bulky face mask and mitt the size of a watermelon, would not catch the ball. The title "catcher" was a misnomer because balls usually just bonked off her glove, face mask, or chest protector.

Lisa was the right fielder, which was where fewest balls were hit. I think that maybe two balls were hit into right field all season. However, that did not mean she didn't get to retrieve the ball. Whenever a ball was hit into ANY field—left, center, or right—Lisa would run to get it. Being the fastest person on the team, she almost always got to the ball before the other fielders. Then, to her credit, rather than hurl the ball wildly despite parents' screams of "Throw it! Throw it!" she would carry the ball as she ran back into the infield, chasing the runner around the bases. This was much more effective than throwing it.

For both Lisa and me, playing girls' softball was a welcomed outlet for the stresses of her illness. The physical activity helped burn her excess energy in a positive way and also enabled both of us to sleep much better.

Lisa's imagination and penchant for telling tall tales were honed during the second and third grades. She came upwith some incredible stories. One was about her pet pig. She related during show-and-tell in her class that we had a pet pig named Elmer that lived in our back yard. She obviously felt a need to have the most unusual story to gain some sort of importance or self-esteem among her peers.

We became aware of her story when the teacher called and asked if we could bring the pig to visit the class.

Another time Lisa brought home a turtle that she said she found in the ditch while walking home from school. The next day she took it to school, and one of her classmates screamed, "That's my turtle! You stole my turtle!" You wonder why Lisa would take the turtle to school, knowing it belonged to a classmate. This was an early example of her inability to think ahead and examine consequences. As a second grader, it could be written off as cute. As a teenager and later as an adult, this inability to predict and understand consequences would get her into real trouble.

Then one evening in November the phone rang.

"Is this Lisa's mom?"

"Yes."

"This is Miss Jones, her teacher. I have some good news for you. I spoke to the principal, and he said it would be all right for Lisa to bring her grandfather and his seeing-eye dog to the Grandparents' Day activities."

"What?" I had no idea what she was talking about.

"Lisa explained to us that the reason her grandparents couldn't come to our Grandparents' Day open house and luncheon was that her grandfather was blind and needed a seeing-eye dog, and that since school rules forbid animals on school grounds, they couldn't come."

I explained to the teacher that her grandfather was not blind, and the reason they could not come was because they lived several hours away and could not drive that far. Again, it was imaginative and cute for a seven-year-old, and her dad and I laughed about it. However, something nagged at me in the pit of my stomach. I didn't know it then, but her actions were forming a pattern that would escalate into serious adult situations. It was a portent of things to come.

Chapter 10

I Was Supposed to Bring Flowers?

We tried to keep Lisa busy during the summer months, and one of the activities in which we enrolled her during the summer was a dance class in which she took ballet and tap lessons. She did quite well in these classes, and we all looked forward to the end-of-summer recital where she was scheduled to perform in two group routines. She had a cute red, white, and blue sailor-like costume for a patriotic tap dance number and was dressed like a bumblebee for her other number, a ballet routine.

I took her backstage before the performance and turned her over to a stage mother who was chaperoning the girls. Then I proceeded to the auditorium and found my husband, who had already gone in to save good seats for us.

About five minutes later, a harried and frazzled stage mother burst into the auditorium and hurried over to me exclaiming, "Lisa's sailor hat fell into the toilet!" I wasn't sure what I could do at this point, so I merely replied, "Well, tell her to fish it out and put it on her head because the show must go on!"

About twenty minutes into the show, it was time for Lisa's group tap number. Onto the stage came Lisa, but no hat—the only one without a hat. Lisa had refused to wear it, hoping that, without a hat, she wouldn't have to go out on stage. Her plan didn't work because the stage mother said she could dance without a hat.

Despite her efforts to avoid dancing, she performed her dance with a minimum of mis-steps, and most of the other girls' hats fell off during the dance anyway. To her surprise, she enjoyed being on stage, and she eagerly waited for her next number as a bumblebee.

The bumblebee ballet number went well and was very cute and funny. Her costume was a yellow tutu and black tights with bumblebee wings and antennae. A few more numbers by other groups followed, and the recital was over.

Her first recital was over, except that it wasn't. Unfortunately, I had never taken dance lessons, so I was not prepared for what happened after the recital.

As Lisa's dad and I waited for the dancers to come out after the recital finished, I became concerned. I saw other parents waiting with teddy bears, flowers, balloons, candy, and other child-appropriate gifts.

I turned to David and said, "Oh, no. We don't have anything for her. I didn't know we were supposed to." I walked over to a mom who was also not carrying a gift of any kind and asked her about the other moms who were holding flowers and other items. The mom said she didn't know about bringing anything either because this was her first recital, too. Lisa's dad brushed off my concerns and assured me that it was "no big deal."

It turned out to be a big deal for Lisa. When she and the other girls came running out, I opened my arms and hugged her, telling her she was the best dancer in her class. However, she noticed almost immediately that other girls were receiving gifts from their parents, and she literally "pitched a fit." She screamed and cried that she was the only one who didn't get anything. I explained that I didn't know about the tradition of giving flowers after a performance and that there were other little girls who had not received anything either.

She continued crying loudly and stomping her feet, so we hurried out the door as people were beginning to stare. Her dad was angry because she had made such a scene for, as he called it, "something so stupid." I was upset with myself because I thought I should have somehow known about the tradition, and I was upset with her dance teacher, whom I felt should have said something. *After all, she had had no trouble asking me for the $60 for the costumes.*

Many years later, after Lisa was diagnosed with borderline personality disorder, I looked back on this event and understood why she had been so upset. Her perception of rejection implied to her that she had been "bad" and created intense abandonment fears and inappropriate anger. In her mind, the fact that she didn't get flowers was an indication that she was being rejected by the two people, her dad and me, she trusted most.

It was a classic borderline personality disorder episode, but all I knew at the time was that I didn't know how to control my own child. I thought she was just headstrong and willful and required more discipline. Those conclusions were so wrong.

Oh, how she and I could have benefitted at that time from an accurate diagnosis and appropriate help!

Chapter 11

Cruise Capers

With the end of third grade came more testing. Because Lisa was still having difficulty concentrating and at our insistence, her third grade teacher recommended that the school district department of special programs give her a comprehensive individual assessment to see if she might qualify as learning disabled for some special education services in fourth grade.

However, because her educational performance was at a third- to fourth-grade level in math, spelling, language, and writing, and her reading comprehension was at a sixth grade level, the examiner concluded that she did not have a learning disability as defined by the Texas Education Association. She further determined that "Lisa's educational needs centered on behavioral issues due to distractibility and inattention, which cause her to fall behind in academic work."

Her final recommendation was that Lisa's needs could best be met in the regular classroom with support by the resource teacher. *Can we say, "Falling through the cracks" again?* She didn't have enough difficulty to require special help, but she was having too much difficulty for a regular setting. So, she would start fourth grade in a regular classroom again, and I braced myself for another year of steady trips to the school for conferences.

Needing to re-charge ourselves, Lisa's dad and I felt we had to get away before fourth grade began, so we planned a seven-day Alaska cruise. We arranged for Brian to stay with my mom and dad on their farm. He loved it there, and they loved having him. Lisa was too much of a handful for them, so we planned for Lisa to stay with Granny, David's mom.

When we asked Granny if she would take care of Lisa for a week while we went on a cruise, she replied, "Oh, I've always wanted to go on a cruise. I'll pay for the kids' fares and help you take care of them if you let me go with you."

It was not quite what I had in mind for a vacation, but we agreed and the five of us (David, Granny, Brian, Lisa, and I) set sail for our Alaska cruise. *I had really wanted for just the two of us—David and me—to get away, but what was I supposed to do? Tell an old woman she couldn't fulfill a dream from her bucket list?*

Fortunately, there was a children's program on the ship, so during the day Lisa kept busy with putt-putt golf, tee shirt painting, and games. At mealtimes, however, she was with us, and she had no patience at all for the leisurely fine dining of a cruise ship. She refused to eat anything but French fries. She fidgeted constantly and inappropriately interacted with the wait staff by hugging them and pulling on their jackets. She refused to eat with a knife and fork and aggravated her brother constantly by stealing his silverware or napkin or punching him in the arm. She blurted out in a loud voice, "I'm hungry," or "Why can't they hurry?" or "When is the food going to come?" She would grab the dinner knife and try to dig holes into the table.

I often took her back to our cabin to calm her down so the rest of the family could eat in peace and without the stares of people at neighboring tables.

She acted like a two-year-old in a nine-year-old's body. I didn't know what to do to help my child. It was impossible to discipline her. I felt hopeless, and I blamed myself. Guilt settled in and became a constant companion.

One evening, however, I received an unexpected compliment about Lisa. Her youth counselor came up to me and told me how much she appreciated what Lisa had done that day. *Well, this was a new one—someone seeking me out to praise Lisa!*

The counselor went on to relate what had happened during the youth scavenger hunt earlier. The group divided into teams, but one of the youths was developmentally handicapped, and none of the others wanted her as a partner. Lisa stepped up and said, "I'll be her partner!" and off they went, Lisa racing ahead with the list of objects to find, with her mentally handicapped friend in tow. They were quite successful, too, and managed to win second place. The counselor was extremely grateful to Lisa for her gesture.

We would hear similar stories about Lisa championing the underdog in future years. Helping others less fortunate seemed to give her a sense of identity and self-esteem. Many years later we discovered there was an actual biological basis for this. Researchers found that the act of helping others releases a chemical called dopamine, which acts as an anxiety-reducer. The chemical structure of the brains of individuals with certain neurological disorders such as OCD, ADHD, and BPD are particularly susceptible to dopamine's effects.

Chapter 12

Foiled Again

Fourth grade began with Lisa again in a regular classroom setting. Since we couldn't get special placement in school due to educational needs, we tried another avenue. Four weeks into fourth grade, during our second conference with her frustrated teacher, we asked that Lisa be referred for a psychological evaluation to determine whether she met the Texas Education Agency guidelines as seriously emotionally disturbed. Her grades had fallen from B's and C's the previous year to failing nearly every subject.

Her fourth-grade teacher was happy to help by explicitly describing Lisa's behaviors in the classroom for the referral:

- She is easily distracted, inattentive, does not always face the task at hand.
- She handles objects on her desk constantly, plays with her clothing, and tips her chair back.
- She asks unrelated questions, does not follow directions, and fails to complete tasks.
- She pulls her eyelashes and picks at sores.
- She complies with teacher requests, but seems purposely slow.

- She is popular with the other students and has many friends.
- She does much better in one-on-one situations, in preferential seating, or in isolation when doing her work.
- She "borrows" things off the teacher's desk without permission.
- Her perceptions are distorted and she acts out impulsively.
- She is under the care of a psychiatrist and psychologist and currently is taking Ritalin and Anafranil for her diagnosed ADHD and nervous habits.

I was certain that these documented observations by her teacher—after only four weeks of school—would qualify her to be put into a classroom more conducive to her type of learning.

Again, however, much to our surprise and disappointment, the psychological report concluded that "Lisa does not qualify as seriously emotionally disturbed according to TEA guidelines" because she was attentive and appropriate in the one-on-one testing situation.   *Hel-lo! Did the teacher not say that she did well in one-on-one but couldn't function in a classroom? Naturally, she will seem functional when she is the sole object of attention from the test administrator.*

The recommendation from the department of special programs went on to say this: "Unfortunately, Lisa is a student who could easily 'fall between the cracks' *(there it is again)* in the school system. She does not qualify for resource help but does need extra attention. Teachers should give her extra attention as much as possible in the regular classroom." *I don't know who was more disappointed—us or her teacher.*

Her grades continued to fall dramatically as the fourth grade continued. She seemed to be trying deliberately to fail and was indeed in danger of doing so. It wasn't until one of her counseling sessions with Dr. Merle that she explained her conduct. She said that everyone had told her that fifth grade would be really hard, so she was trying to fail fourth grade so that she could repeat it instead of being promoted to fifth grade.

This was another clue that Lisa's problems were beyond the diagnosis of ADHD or even oppositional defiant disorder, which had once been thrown out there as a possible diagnosis. She was exhibiting difficulty in thinking processes called executive functioning skills, which included logic and the ability to think ahead and anticipate consequences. It is an "invisible disability" of poor judgment that is often mistaken for laziness or carelessness.

This was a problem that a special education teacher would have been trained to identify and deal with. Unfortunately, Lisa had not qualified for special education, and we wasted almost an entire school year struggling. *Fell through the cracks again.*

Chapter 13

Highs and Lows

Fifth grade was a complex challenge for the entire family. Lisa was unable to adjust to the fact that her dad and I were separated and getting a divorce.

Her dad had moved out of our home on the east side of Houston and into an apartment about a mile away, where Lisa and her brother visited him two evenings a week and every other weekend.

He soon was unable to cope with Lisa's escalating antics and told her, "Lisa, I can't handle both you and the divorce at the same time." He began to modify the visits by her and her brother, letting them visit one at a time instead of together.

Their visits to their father were welcomed breaks in my constant anxiety over Lisa. It was becoming more and more difficult to deal with her, and I began to fear that she would keep behaving this way forever.

Lisa's impulsiveness and erratic behaviors were increasing, both at home and at school. She frustrated easily and threw tantrums. The mood swings were sudden. One minute she would be happy, and the next minute she would be angry and upset for no apparent reason. At school she became bored quickly with tasks and was easily distracted. She was very active and could not keep still. She blurted out comments and could never wait for turns or share.

Her Ritalin dosage was increased for the third time, and her behavior improved a bit. However, she then added something new to her repertoire of undesirable behaviors.

She began to steal money. There were times that I just knew I had had a twenty-dollar bill in my wallet, but it was gone. Another time, a cousin at our family reunion told me she had seen Lisa taking money out of some purses. I later learned that she had also been taking money from fifth-grade classmates at school.

The demands of Lisa's actions exhausted me, both physically and mentally. Her inability to "listen and obey" was particularly frustrating, and my knowledge of the potential consequences of her behaviors was making me anxious and stressed. Also, the stark difference between my personality and Lisa's made her behavior especially difficult to accept. My frustration was leading to anger—and guilt about being angry at my child.

I also worried about my son, Brian. I feared that his needs were getting less attention than Lisa's and that his accomplishments were being overshadowed by his sister's demands on my time. I feared he would develop resentful feelings toward his sister—and toward me.

Lisa would physically hit him, but, being older and male, he insisted on being a "gentleman" and wouldn't hit her back.

At the suggestion of Lisa's doctor, I decided to seek treatment for myself to learn how to deal with her symptoms, my inner conflicts, and my failed marriage. I began seeing a therapist who was committed to helping me deal with my own life in a healthy manner.

His first piece of advice was this: "Take care of yourself. When you take care of yourself, you are better able to take care of your child." As my child's role model and most important source of strength, he advised me to eat right, exercise, and try to reduce stress, whether it is by taking a warm bath or a long walk. He told me to remember that Lisa's behavior related to a disorder and was not intentional and certainly not my fault.

Inwardly I knew these things, but I was so insecure at this point that I needed to hear them from someone else.

L isa had few real friends—the kind that would invite her to their homes for sleepovers, invite her to birthday parties, etc. Most parents had become aware of her behavior problems and would exclude her from social activities out of school. Although I could understand their reasons, it still made me angry and disappointed and a little embarrassed. I don't know if Lisa ever realized how many parties and sleep-overs she missed because I tried to keep her busy with family activities.

Lisa did have one loyal friend named Ashley. Ashley seemed to be able to understand Lisa, be patient with her, and forgive her storytelling (lying). They spent a lot of time together, and Ashley has remained a true friend for many years.

The increase in her medication seemed to be helping Lisa control her impulses and energy. To help her work off some of her still-elevated energy levels, I enrolled Lisa in a Taekwondo class at the local community center. We bought a gi (traditional uniform), and she went to three lessons before the instructor called me to say that he didn't think the class was working out for Lisa. When I pressed him as to why, he hesitantly replied something like, "She doesn't seem to want to participate."

When I asked Lisa if she was having problems in the class, she responded, "I don't like punching and kicking. The only thing I like about the lessons is the sweet rice candy we get after class." That was the end of Taekwondo for her. I looked for something else.

I signed her up for a babysitting class at the local YMCA. She loved children and was anxious to be certified as a babysitter. I knew she could not be trusted to babysit for awhile yet, but I felt as if the training would be useful and a source of accomplishment for Lisa. She did well in the class and received her babysitting certification.

Another successful endeavor was a modeling class for ten- to twelve-year-olds, sponsored by Macy's at a nearby shopping mall. It was an eight-week class on weekends, and Lisa had a lot of fun learning social skills, poise, and confidence while doing age-appropriate modeling. The final day of the program was a fashion show for the public to showcase the students' accomplishments, and she really did a great job, gracefully modeling several outfits. She had the perfect body for modeling, as she was tall and thin, and she seemed comfortable on stage with no stage fright at all. She also loved the fact that she could keep the outfits that she modeled.

It was a positive, esteem-enhancing experience for both of us, and I was beginning to feel cautiously optimistic that she would "grow out" of her behavior problems.

It didn't take long, however, for my hopefulness to be dashed, leaving me once more in tears, disappointed and angry. The situation involved a fifth-grade school trip.

For many years, the fifth grade class in Lisa's elementary school had taken a five-day trip to Washington, D.C. My son, Brian, had gone several years prior when he was in fifth grade and had had a wonderful, fun, educational experience. Naturally, when the note came home that all parents of students interested in the upcoming fifth-grade Washington, D.C. trip should attend a meeting at the school cafeteria, I marked it on my calendar.

I arrived at the meeting early, filled out the information packet, picked up a flyer and other information about the trip, and sat down, waiting for the meeting to begin.

Just as the meeting was about to start, and in front of a cafeteria full of parents, the assistant principal came over to me, leaned down, and whispered loudly, "I'm afraid that Lisa will not be allowed to go on the school trip."

Shocked, I responded, "But, why?"

The assistant principal, in an even louder whisper, said, "Because we are only taking students with good conduct records, and Lisa's conduct in school has not been good enough for us to take her on the trip."

Still in disbelief, I told her, "But I am willing to pay my own way and go along as a chaperone to help out."

"No, I'm sorry," she said, "so there is no need for you to stay at tonight's meeting. You can contact the principal tomorrow if you have any further questions."

I got up to go, still shocked, but the shock turned to embarrassment and shame as I walked across the room in front of all of those parents with kids who behaved well in school. I could feel their eyes looking at me, some with pity and some with arrogance. I felt my face flush.

On the drive home, my embarrassment turned to anger. I was livid that the school administration had not screened the list of fifth graders before the invitations to the meeting were mailed. That way I would have known in advance that Lisa was not going to be allowed on the trip and would not have been embarrassed in front of all the other parents.

Why was I embarrassed? I was embarrassed because those looks from the other parents made me feel as if I were a bad mother. The looks said to me, "If only you were a better parent, your child could have gone on the trip."

The next day, I tried to call the principal, but he didn't return my call. Meanwhile, I had to tell Lisa that she wasn't going to Washington, D.C. Her response was surprising. Though she had been looking forward to the trip, she simply said that it was okay, and that maybe we could go as a family sometime.

She clearly wasn't having as much difficulty with the decision as I was, so I chose not to persist in trying to reach the principal. Instead, I stewed in my own conflicting emotions for several days, not knowing whether to feel sadness, anger, embarrassment, hopelessness, or resignation. Or all five. Mostly I just had a vague sense that I was doing everything wrong and that I was inadequate for the task of parenting Lisa.

Chapter 14

Holding and Hypnosis

I was desperate to help my child fit into society, so over the next few months, I tried two "alternative" therapies I had heard about, not aware of the disastrous results that, but for the grace of God, could have resulted.

I discovered the first non-traditional therapy during one of my master's degree classes at the University of Houston—Clear Lake, in which I sat next to a master's candidate in psychotherapy. He told me about an attachment-disorder therapist for whom he worked that specialized in "holding therapy." He explained that holding therapy is a treatment used primarily with fostered or adopted children who have behavioral difficulties ascribed to an inability to attach to parents because of their suppressed rage from abandonment by their natural mother.

Advocates of this type of treatment also believe that emotional attachment of a child to an adoptive parent is affected by the child's prenatal period, during which the unborn child is aware of the natural mother's thoughts and emotions. If the natural mother is distressed by the pregnancy, especially if she considers abortion, the child responds with distress and anger that continue to express themselves throughout the child's life.

Because Lisa is adopted, her father and I felt that there might be something to this. We were ready to try anything.

I made an appointment with the holding therapist, who, to her credit, first did an evaluation of Lisa. She determined that Lisa's problems did not stem from an attachment disorder, so she did not recommend holding therapy. However, we continued to see her for regular psychotherapy counseling for several months.

Since then, holding therapy has been criticized and debunked by the scientific community. This type of therapy utilizes restraint and confrontation to produce in the child a rage response with the goal of achieving catharsis. The child is physically restrained and firmly held (or lain upon) by therapists until the child stops resisting.

Indeed, it is now considered to be a very dangerous treatment because there have been a number of cases of serious harm to and even death of children who received extreme forms of holding therapy. Today, only a handful of clinics in the U.S. utilize this coercive form of therapy.

The next type of unconventional treatment was hypnotism. A parent in the waiting room of our therapist mentioned that she knew of a hypnosis therapist that worked with children who had severe behavioral difficulties. I asked for his name and called for an appointment.

The psychiatric hypnotist was not located in Houston, but rather in Corpus Christi, Texas, about a four-hour drive away. Lisa and I drove there the night before our 9:00 a.m. appointment and stayed in a hotel. We pretended it was a sleepover, and we watched TV and ate pizza.

The next morning, we drove to the psychiatrist's office in downtown Corpus Christi. There was no receptionist, so I pressed a buzzer, and we waited until the doctor appeared.

The doctor was a slight man, about sixty years old with gray hair, who had a comfortable presence and a pleasant demeanor.

He welcomed us into his office and then explained how psychiatric hypnotherapy has been known to break negative patterns of behavior, such as impulsive behavior.

He went on to tell us that the hypnotic state is not as mysterious as it sounds. People go into trancelike states all the time. For example, musicians and artists can become so engrossed in their work that they lose track of time. Readers often become totally immersed in the pages of a good book. Drivers pass their exits on the freeway while daydreaming. These day-to-day experiences are similar to the hypnotic state.

I insisted on staying in the room with Lisa as she began the process of relaxation into the first of three stages, the superficial trance. At this point, her eyes were closed, but she was still very aware of her surroundings. Unfortunately, for whatever reason, she was not able to progress to the next, deeper stage. The doctor suggested she go into the waiting room to play for awhile and then return to try again later.

In the meantime, he suggested that I try some relaxation therapy to help with my stress and emotional tension. I sat in a chair while he stood behind me and massaged my temples as I did some breathing exercises.

His hands slid from my temples to my shoulders, which he massaged gently. I was so relaxed that it took a couple of moments for me to realize that his hands had migrated to my breasts and were caressing them. I jumped up from the chair and exclaimed, "What are you doing?"

I didn't really wait for an answer, as I quickly grabbed my purse and bolted out the door into the waiting room where Lisa was playing with some toys. I grabbed her by the hand, shoved her into the car, and I began driving home.

I was practically speechless for the entire trip, as I tried to process what had just happened. I didn't say anything to Lisa about what had happened although she was curious about why we had left in such a hurry. I simply said that we had made a mistake going to see this man.

I wanted to report the doctor's actions to someone, but I didn't know to whom. I knew that if I filed a formal complaint with the licensing board, it would be his word against mine and could get messy. I finally confided in an attorney friend, who said he would do some checking.

He reported to me the following week that the doctor's phone had been disconnected and his office had been closed.

I never told anyone else about what happened.

Chapter 15

Mom, I Forgot How to Stop

During Lisa's fifth grade, her dad and I were in the final stages of getting a divorce. During this time, I met Bill, a fellow professor at the college, whom I began seeing socially. Lisa liked Bill because he was very good to her, and she liked having the extra attention.

It was late in the school year during spring break when Bill took the three of us—Lisa, Brian, and me—on a skiing trip to a family-friendly resort near Santa Fe, New Mexico. We were all having a wonderful time, and both Lisa and Brian were taking skiing lessons.

On our last day, Lisa was attempting to ski downhill on a suitably graded beginners' slope. Bill and I were waiting at the bottom of the hill when we saw several medical personnel hurrying up the hill.

Something—maybe mother's intuition—told me that the person in trouble was Lisa. I raced up the hill to where she was lying motionless in the snow in her bright yellow ski outfit. One leg, still attached to the ski, was stretched in front of her, and the other was curled under her. My heart drummed fear against my ribcage.

She was conscious and called out, "Mommy, I forgot how to stop!" when she saw me. The paramedics instructed her to remain very still as they immobilized her neck and back, while trying to get a clear picture of what happened.

Several onlookers who saw her fall reported that it looked as if her skis got tangled together, causing her to fly through the air, head over heels, landing on her neck and head. One of the ladies added, "It was a horrible and scary landing."

The paramedics then questioned Lisa about having any radiating pain, numbness, or tingling in her extremities. She responded that she had sharp pains in her neck and upper shoulder. They checked her sensation by lightly touching her arms and legs, and she said she could feel everything. They continued their evaluation by having her move her toes and fingers.

These were all encouraging signs, but the EMS personnel felt she should be evaluated by a neurologist at the nearby hospital. They explained that a spinal injury cannot be ruled out even if the patients can feel their limbs.

They carried her down the mountain by sled and then carefully loaded her onto an ambulance. I climbed inside with her, and Bill prepared to follow in our car. I sat by her side and held her hand tightly. I prayed fervently as the ambulance flew down the curvy mountainous road, siren wailing, toward Santa Fe Hospital. Seeing Bill through the back window of the ambulance as he followed in hot pursuit was my only comfort.

My strangely calm daughter was immediately examined and x-rayed at the emergency room, but it seemed like years before the neurologist returned to her bedside and reported that the x-rays showed no spinal injuries. She had a serious sprain but she would be fine. She probably had some stretched tendons and ligaments and would have two or three days of acute pain and swelling, followed by slow healing and a gradual reduction of pain.

It was the first ambulance ride for both Lisa and me, but what we didn't know then was that there would be dozens more ambulance trips in the coming years. *I'm glad we didn't know that at the time.*

The next day, we drove to the airport to fly home, but the excitement of the trip wasn't finished.

Our Boeing 727 had just lifted off and was ascending toward its cruising altitude when we felt and heard a loud "thump." The plane jolted and then began to vibrate as the putrid smell of burning feathers filled the cabin. There wasn't a sound in the hushed cabin as the passengers became eerily quiet.

Then a frightened little voice broke the silence, "Mama, are we going to fall?" The voice was Lisa's. She had verbalized what every person on that plane was silently asking.

Before I could respond to her, the captain began speaking over the intercom and informed us that one of the engines seemed to have ingested a goose that was migrating in the area. The bird strike, he said, had disabled one engine, so we were going to return to Santa Fe. He asked us to remain calm because the crew was highly trained in landing aircraft with only one engine.

We did, indeed, land uneventfully and were put on the next flight to Houston, much to the frustration of passengers booked on that flight, who were bumped onto later flights.

Chapter 16

New Life, New School

I married Bill later that year, when Lisa was eleven years old and about to enter sixth grade. The children and I had been living in a suburb of Houston on its far east side, and Bill had lived on the far west side of the city. We decided that we would live in Bill's home, even though it meant uprooting the children, because we wanted to enroll Lisa in an acclaimed private school in his area for children with learning disabilities and developmental problems. Bill's son had attended this school with considerable success, and we hoped it might be the answer for Lisa's problems as well.

We applied to the school as soon as we all settled into our new home, but after an interview, Lisa was not accepted into the school. The administrators felt that her emotional problems were not appropriate for placement in their curriculum.

I was devastated. *Another door slammed in our faces.*

The school year was about to begin, so we had no choice but to enroll Lisa into the nearby public intermediate school. We provided the school with all of Lisa's psychological testing results and her complete school and medical history. We asked for modifications similar to those she had received in fifth grade, where for example, she was required to do fewer math problems than the rest of the class. We explained that this type of modification had proved very successful, as Lisa tended to become overwhelmed and give up when she had lengthy assignments. When given shortened assignments, her work was almost always completely accurate.

Unfortunately, the public intermediate school refused to provide the accommodations that had worked in elementary school and informed us that they preferred to observe Lisa's performance themselves during the first months of school before deciding about modifications. She was placed in a regular sixth grade program.

I was frustrated that years of testing, experience, and experimental teaching methods would be ignored by the school as they tried to "re-invent the wheel."

My fears were confirmed as Lisa's difficulties began almost immediately. She refused to do her work in the classroom, often turning in blank sheets. On one occasion she wrote a suicide note and passed it around in class, frightening several of the other students.

She refused to follow directions and constantly distracted other students in the classroom, relishing the self-imposed title of class clown. She stole keys from one teacher's purse and forty dollars from another teacher's purse on separate occasions. She also stole a calculator from a student, skipped classes, and was tardy or truant on multiple occasions. She had dozens of discipline referrals, detention halls (which she rarely attended), and of course, failing grades on her report card. She was tardy to most of her classes nearly every day.

This was all in the first six weeks of the sixth grade.

Throughout this period, we were attending weekly sessions with Lisa's psychologist, Dr. German, who explained that Lisa was trying to cope with a "perfect storm" of recent emotional upsets.

First, there was the divorce and my subsequent re-marriage, followed immediately by moving to a new home in another part of the city. This meant starting a new school and having to make new friends.

Further complicating the scenario was the fact that she was now in middle school, which had fewer restrictions and more freedom than elementary school. She now changed classrooms and had different teachers for each subject rather than the consistent environment of one classroom and one teacher.

It made perfect sense, but knowing what was contributing to her problems helped little in dealing with the repercussions, and I still felt like the worst parent in the world.

After six weeks of turmoil, the intermediate school principal finally agreed with us that Lisa definitely required modifications for her education that only special education could provide. He said he had been reluctant to consider special education because many parents accept special education only as a last resort because of the lifetime of stigma they associate with it. However, there was no other option we could find that would allow Lisa to learn successfully.

We began the process of qualifying for special education all over again. Just as before, she needed a variety of testing, a comprehensive individual assessment by the school district, referrals from doctors, and lengthy questionnaires and interviews.

We were told that the school district would provide all of the testing needed. However, there was just one catch. So many students needed to be evaluated that there was a huge backlog, and Lisa couldn't be tested until February, which was five months away. We wanted to start the ball rolling immediately, so we arranged for private evaluations that could be completed sooner. These would be costly to us (the school district testing was free), but we felt that we had no time to waste.

In late September, she underwent an evaluation by a speech and language pathologist, who administered a battery of nine tests to evaluate Lisa's general intellectual capabilities and language learning functioning.

After the testing, the pathologist told us that my daughter's social skills were more like those of a seven-year-old than those of a twelve-year-old. One example: Lisa had picked up a doll from a sofa in the office, held it throughout the session, and talked to it.

The pathologist, however, also said that Lisa was cooperative and had a reasonable attention span (she had taken her Ritalin just before the evaluation). On the other hand, as the medication began to wear off, after about two and a half hours of testing, there were definite changes in her behavior, particularly her inability to maintain attention.

The 23-page report we were given was comprehensive, with graphs and percentiles and psycho-speak, but it was the one-page summary and list of twenty-three recommendations I was most interested in. In summary, the pathologist stated that Lisa had a receptive and expressive language disorder. *I have a master's degree, but I had no idea what those terms meant in practical terms.*

The pathologist gave us some examples. Lisa couldn't remember concepts because she couldn't understand them. She couldn't formulate complex sentences or create complex explanations because she had difficulty with abstract words such as "until," "although," and "even if." She could write a simple story, but could not develop ideas as someone of her age should be expected to do. She couldn't spell because she had poor visual memory.

Her math skills were the weakest. She had difficulty recalling multiplication facts, the number of days in a year, number of weeks in a year, and so on.

The clinician further explained that children with such poor pragmatic language skills often cope with these difficulties by withdrawing from social situations with peers and instead seeking out much younger children for playmates, children with similar skills. They also become masters at avoidance. If solving a problem is difficult, it is easier to give up than to try.

Lisa also had difficulty understanding possible causes for problems. One of the situations presented to her during the evaluation was this: "The losing baseball team has just lost three games in a row. What could they do to improve the way they play?" Lisa's response was, "Practice."

I think that was a good response. I might have said the same thing.

The evaluator, however, felt that the response was too succinct and incomplete. *What was she supposed to say—"Fire the manager and trade for Babe Ruth?"*

Another response that the pathologist felt was extremely simplistic was when she was asked why people in a pictured scene decided to go to a restaurant. Lisa replied, "to eat." The pathologist felt that someone of Lisa's age should have answered, "to celebrate a special occasion," "to try a new restaurant," or "they didn't feel like cooking."

Some of her other responses were obviously inappropriate, such as her response to the situation of what a woman should do if she witnesses a minor automobile accident. Lisa responded, "Ask for the insurance company." She clearly misunderstood what "witness" meant. *Okay, so what do we do with all of this information?*

The pathologist recommended that we continue Lisa's psychological counseling as intensively as possible, continue her medication, and start Lisa with regular sessions with a speech and language pathologist to develop better language processing skills. *Okay, no problem. But what about the school?*

Among the eighteen educational recommendations, the pathologist gave excellent, practical, and specific suggestions, such as

• Modify Lisa's curriculum to stress quality rather than quantity. Limit written words required.

- Provide special seating away from distractions and allow her to do something with her hands while listening, such as "doodling."
- Lots of breaks!
- Provide assistance in organizing lockers and binders.
- Positive encouragement.
- Reduce memory load. Instead of asking who the first governor of Texas was, ask, "Who was the first governor of Texas, Sam Houston or Jim Bowie?"
- Modify grading expectations in spelling.

She also offered to work with Lisa's teachers individually.

All in all, she recommended a highly encouraging environment and a severely modified curriculum. *Nothing new here.*

This pathologist, however, came closer than anyone else had previously come in suggesting that there was an underlying brain disorder beyond ADHD. She used the metaphor of Swiss cheese. Using her chalkboard to draw a picture of the brain, she demonstrated that Lisa's brain was like Swiss cheese, with holes in some areas where certain functions occurred. Sometimes, if the nerve pathways don't have to go through a "hole," she functions fine.

Her concern for Lisa was that since her social skills were so immature, as she grew older she would choose friends with poor social skills, which could lead to involvement with drugs and alcohol.

The therapist also felt that Lisa would function best in a class for students with learning disabilities but that she didn't qualify because she had no "quantifiable disability." She could learn under the right circumstances, but those circumstances were not present in a regular classroom setting. *Fell through the cracks again. Not disabled, but can't function in a regular setting.*

She urged us to continue pursuing special education qualification with the school counselor.

Chapter 17

Neighborhood Woes

In addition to school problems, things were going downhill quickly in our new neighborhood, too. I had been delighted when a boy-girl set of nine-year-old twins who lived down the street began coming over to play with Lisa after school. They seemed to enjoy coming over and playing with her and showed up unannounced nearly every day after school.

One day, just the boy twin arrived at the door and wanted to play with Lisa. He bounded up the stairs to discover Lisa already had a friend over, and Lisa told him to go home.

Later that evening, I answered the phone to hear his mother on the other end screaming at me, "Your daughter has molested my son, and I want you to come over here immediately!"

Bill and I dropped everything and hurried over. As soon as she opened the door, she laid into us with a barrage of verbal attacks. When I finally had an opening to ask what her son had told her, she said that Lisa and her friend had undressed her son to look at his private parts. She raved that her son had been scarred for life and that she was taking him to counseling, telling everyone in the neighborhood what had happened, and possibly filing legal proceedings against us.

She was still ranting as we walked out of her home. Bill was unemotional, but I was in tears, humiliated. Of course, I confronted Lisa and her friend, who denied everything, saying the boy was just mad that they wouldn't play with him. Wanting to believe my child, I didn't really know what to believe or how much importance to give the episode. I just knew it wasn't a good way to start out in a new neighborhood.

I described the incident to her psychologist Dr. German at our next session, and she brushed it off, saying kids are naturally curious at that age, and that even if it had happened as the boy said, it was no big deal.

We never spoke with this neighbor again, about this incident or about anything else. Although she lives just down the street, we have managed to avoid each other for almost twenty years. No one else in the neighborhood ever indicated they knew about the incident, and we received no legal threats from her lawyer.

There were more troubling events in the neighborhood, and we knew Lisa was probably guilty of them, but other neighbors were kinder and more understanding. On one occasion, Lisa stole forty dollars from Betty down the street, and upon confrontation, admitted it.

When I offered to pay Betty back, she refused and suggested that Lisa instead work off the debt by doing chores for her—natural consequences. So, Lisa went over there after school for several days to wash Betty's car, sweep the driveway, and bathe Betty's dog. I am still grateful to that wonderful lady for her understanding and forgiveness.

Chapter 18

Lose-Lose Situation

A few months after moving in, I found an essay that Brian had written at the beginning of ninth grade in his new school. It was his response to an assignment called "Reflections" and was titled "Little Sister."

"Sisters are like days of the week. Sometimes they're good, and sometimes they are bad.

My sister's name is Lisa. She is three years younger than I am. She is tall and skinny and has medium length brown hair. She loves animals and loves to talk on the phone.

In most ways she is totally opposite from me. She is very outgoing and talkative. When we first moved here this summer, a neighbor told us that Lisa came over and acted like she had known them for ten years. She also gets into a lot of trouble at school for talking. She's also hyperactive and can't sit still.

She drives me crazy most of the time, but sometimes she can be nice. For example, when I'm babysitting an infant, she changes the diapers for me. The other day she spent hours with a baby calf on my granny's farm that had been born sick and later died. Several years ago when we were on a cruise, Lisa befriended a developmentally disabled girl and played with her when no one else would. All in all, sometimes she can be a totally different person from the terror she usually is.

Despite all her faults, I love my sister anyway. I miss her when she's not around. And yet when she is, I wish she would go away. So, I guess in a way it's a lose-lose situation."

Brian earned an A on the essay. More importantly, I gained valuable insight into his feelings about his sister.

Chapter 19

Sibling Caregivers

As Lisa's sibling, Brian was right in the thick of our family struggles with Lisa's behavior. Three and a half years older than Lisa, sometimes he was pulled into the challenging role of caregiver when Bill and I went out for an evening.

An activity and escape from parenting that we enjoyed was square dancing. One evening in the middle of an "allemande left" I glanced at the entry to the dance hall and was shocked to see Brian standing there alongside Lisa. Bill and I finished the dance set, which was almost over, and walked over to them.

"Why are you two here?" I asked, more confused than worried, although Lisa did seem to be in some anguish.

Brian replied calmly but sarcastically, "Lisa thought it would be a good idea to put your contact lenses in her eyes, and now she can't get them out."

"Lisa!" I admonished. "Why would you want to put my contacts in your eyes?"

Expecting the usual "I don't know" from her, she instead responded, "I have watched you put your contacts in your eyes all your life and wanted to see what it was like. Now I don't know how to get them out, and Mommy, it hurts so bad." I escorted her into the ladies' room and examined her eyes. The hard contact lenses had migrated up under the eyelids. Having experienced the same situation myself on a few occasions, I knew how uncomfortable it was. Carefully, while trying to keep her head from moving every time I touched her eye area, I was able to remove the lenses from both her eyes, which were now red and irritated.

Brian felt terrible and apologized for not watching her more closely and allowing this to happen. He added, "I didn't know what to do because she was howling, saying that it hurt so badly."

I told him that it was okay—no harm done. "It's not your fault," I consoled. "Lisa can get into trouble faster than a two-year-old." *And often acts like one.*

On another occasion while we were out square dancing and Brian was at home with his twelve-year-old sister, Lisa suddenly went into an intense emotional rage. She was cursing, yelling, and throwing things. Then she went into the kitchen and took a carving knife out of a drawer.

Before she could threaten herself or Brian with it, he grabbed her and wrestled the knife out of her hand. Then he managed to pin her arms behind her and drag her with him to the telephone, which he used to call his stepsister Cyndie, Bill's daughter, for help.

While waiting for his stepsister, Brian, who was eight inches taller and fifty pounds heavier than Lisa, forced her to lie prone on the kitchen floor while he straddled her to hold her down. He said it was the only way he could keep her from hurting him or herself. *It reminded me of holding therapy when he later told me this.*

According to Brian, Lisa had already calmed down somewhat when Cyndie arrived. She de-escalated even further when she realized that Cyndie had dropped everything and driven twenty minutes from her home just to help out. Lisa promised Cyndie that she would stay calm, take her medication, and go to bed if Brian allowed her to get up. As Lisa was preparing for bed, Cyndie and Brian quickly searched the kitchen for all knives and hid them.

Cyndie agreed to stay with Brian until we returned home. When Bill and I arrived, the house was quiet, but as soon as we saw Cyndie, we knew the entire evening had probably not been as quiet.

Chapter 20

Pavlov's Dog?

In early November, five weeks after Lisa's speech and language appraisal, her psychological evaluation was done by Dr. Joan Rios. This was her third complete psych evaluation in six years. Dr. Rios's report reiterated many of the speech pathologist's findings as well as earlier psychological assessment findings. She also discovered new, unexplainable behaviors.

Repeating the speech evaluation's findings, Dr. Rios noted that Lisa acted and looked much younger than her twelve years of age. For example, she raided the candy jar continuously until asked to stop, and she sat inappropriately with her legs far apart in a way that would embarrass most twelve-year-old girls. However, just as the pathologist had commented, at no time was her behavior obnoxious or rude.

Her testing again showed that Lisa interprets her environment incorrectly and with the skills of a seven-year-old. The doctor was perplexed, however, about Lisa's test behavior, which was more like children who have attachment disorder. This was not consistent with Dr. Rios's certainty that Lisa has bonded with and has great trust in me. Her story-telling was of concern to the doctor because in many of her stories either an animal or person was dying or was killed. Dr. Rios interpreted this as a fear Lisa had of not being protected or cared for.

The psychologist's recommendations were the same as the ones the speech pathologist had given: continue medication, continue psychotherapy, and provide structure, routine, and monitoring in school. She added, in no uncertain terms, that Lisa must have an individualized education plan (IEP) or she "would not make it."

She was equally strong in her position that punishment was not the proper method of discipline because, due to Lisa's inability to process properly, she would not understand why she was being punished and would simply feel abused and unwanted.

The doctor suggested natural consequences, such as repayment of money stolen, and constant repeating of lessons and rules because "Lisa cannot internalize them and must learn them by conditioning—like Pavlov's dog."

Dr. Rios then took me by the hand, looked me directly in the eye, and said, "Linda, I want you to know that you are doing a super job as a mother. You are a super mother. You have been a super mother all these years, and you have been very patient."

Strangely enough, that didn't make me feel much better. My daughter was still in trouble despite my best efforts.

There was yet another issue that I didn't know how to deal with. I didn't know if it was related to her other problems or not, but Lisa had been suffering from nocturnal enuresis (bedwetting) all her life. It was very embarrassing for her, and I must admit that I was not always patient with her. I often moaned an "Oh, no, why didn't you go to the bathroom!" when I came upstairs to wake her for school and discovered that her bed sheets were soaked in urine. I'm sure that didn't make her feel any better about it.

We had tried several things, including setting an alarm for the middle of the night so we could take her to the bathroom. Nothing seemed to work, and the problem made it nearly impossible for her to sleep over at a friend's house.

I told her doctor that she was a very heavy sleeper, and he surmised that she probably failed to awaken when her bladder was full. In addition, we were told, her bladder may be smaller than normal, a condition that is hereditary. He stated that most children outgrow this problem by the time they are eighteen.

Eighteen? Another problem to deal with in her volatile adolescence. Not to mention self-esteem and shame issues that Lisa would suffer in the meantime.

Her doctor began prescribing Imipramine at bedtime, which seemed to work most nights. She still had the occasional "accident" about twice a week.

Chapter 21

ARD at Last

Lisa's report card in early November was a disaster. She had F's in science, math, literature, and language arts. Comments in each class included the descriptors "Behavior is a problem," "Too talkative," and "Missing work." I called the school and insisted on an immediate conference. The year was speeding by, and we were still waiting for the school to do something. We had done our part with the language and psychological evaluations, both of which had insisted that Lisa needed special educational accommodations.

In mid-November, I met with the intermediate school counselor, a special education teacher, and four of Lisa's current teachers for a "service review." After two hours of reviewing Lisa's testing, her discipline referrals, and her grades, it was unanimously agreed to convene an ARD committee in early January.

In Texas, an ARD committee (Admission, Review, and Dismissal) is a team made up of a student's parents and school staff who meet to decide whether or not the student has an eligible disability, to determine if special education services will be provided, and to develop an individual education program, or IEP.

In the meantime, Lisa's teachers agreed to implement as many of Dr. Rios's recommendations as possible. She was placed in an "adaptive behavior" classroom for specially-designed instruction in math.

Detentions and discipline continued throughout the remainder of November and all of December. She was still making D's and F's in all of her sixth-grade academic classes, except for resource math class. She related well to the special education math teacher and brought her grades up to a C. In fact, her teacher sent a note to me one day, which read, "Lisa is doing really well, and I enjoy having her in class." *This type of program is what I wanted for all her classes—not just math!*

Although working at a fourth grade level, Lisa felt successful as she was able to solve at least simple math problems. This gave her some small level of self-esteem and resulted in classroom behavior that was on task and not disruptive. Unfortunately, this feeling of success didn't carry over into her other classes or her outside activities.

It was during this time, just before Christmas, that I was called by the manager of a grocery store located a block away from Lisa's school. He told me that Lisa had been caught shoplifting after school. No charges were filed, but she was told by the manager not to ever enter the store again. This was a store where I shopped regularly, but because of my embarrassment, I changed grocery stores.

Verapamil, a medication for treating manic symptoms in bipolar disorder, was added to her growing list of medications, which already included Ritalin for ADHD, Anafranil for anxiety, and Imipramine for bedwetting.

After months of waiting, Lisa's ARD finally convened after Christmas. Lisa's improved behavior in her more structured math setting, her speech/language assessment, and her psychological assessment were reviewed and discussed, and information from her other teachers was shared with the group.

Unfortunately, the committee felt additional testing by the school psychologist "would be beneficial" to determine Lisa's eligibility for special education services.

I wanted to scream, "What else do you need?" More delay. Half the school year was over.

We had already spent our own money to have Lisa privately tested in order to hasten the special education placement so that months of precious learning time wouldn't be lost. Yet they still wanted their own person to do the testing, and we would have to wait anyway.

The committee did, however, agree to place Lisa into two more adaptive behavior classes, pending the results of the school's psychological assessment, after which another ARD would be scheduled. *At least she was now in three modified classes.*

Chapter 22

Knock, Knock, Who's There?

One chilly evening in early February, I was preparing dinner when the doorbell rang. At the door was a middle-aged, well-dressed lady who said she was from Child Protective Services and wanted to speak with me and with Lisa's stepfather. I asked her in, summoned Bill, who was at his desk grading accounting exams, and the three of us sat down in our living room.

The CPS worker began by relating that she had been called by the school nurse to investigate possible child abuse by Lisa's stepfather. Lisa had appeared in the nurse's office earlier that day for her midday medication when the nurse noticed bruising on Lisa's arm.

When the nurse questioned Lisa, Lisa claimed that the bruises had arisen when her stepfather had grabbed her. The nurse pursued the issue by asking Lisa if her stepfather was mean to her. Lisa responded by saying, "Yes, he beats me." The nurse then called Child Protective Services.

Bill and I were stunned.

Bill was so shocked he couldn't say anything. I took a moment to pull myself together, and when I was able to speak, I told the worker, "That is an absolute lie. Bill has never laid a hand on her, except when she was out of control and in danger of hurting herself or others and he had to physically restrain her. But he has never beaten her or even spanked her."

The CPS worker then asked, "Then what do you ascribe her bruises to?"

I sat silent for a moment before responding, "I have no idea because she didn't have them when she left for school this morning."

At this point, I called Lisa down from her upstairs bedroom where she had been since coming home from school. She sauntered into the living room and seemed curious about the visitor but unemotional. Until I explained who the visitor was. Suddenly, Lisa looked shocked, scared, and uncomfortable. I then confronted her with the accusation she had made against Bill.

At first, she didn't respond at all and just stood in the doorway, looking down at her feet. Finally, the CPS worker asked her in a straightforward manner, "Lisa, did your stepfather cause those bruises on your arm?"

It was then that I first noticed the black and blue marks on Lisa's right arm. They seemed to be in a triangular shape about four inches long.

Lisa kept her head lowered and still didn't say anything. The CPS worker repeated her question. Finally, Lisa in a tiny, childlike voice, said, "No."

I blurted out immediately, "Why did you say he did?" followed by, "And where did you get those bruises?"

The first question might as well have been rhetorical because her whiny answer was the same as it has always been when asked why she did something: "I don't know."

As for the bruises, Lisa finally admitted to hitting herself with a piece of lumber she had found so that she could blame her stepfather. She had hoped, she went on, that he would go to jail so that her dad could come back and live with us. With the interpretation skills and maturity of a six-year-old, Lisa had still not been able to grasp the divorce. Her therapist later explained,

"Lisa can't act rationally because she has an inaccurate perception of reality. She tends to view others and herself in 'all or nothing' terms. This is called black-white thinking, or splitting."

She couldn't blame me or her father because to do so would, in her mind, be to hate us. The only person left to hate and blame was Bill. Because to Lisa there were no "gray" gradations between black and white, someone was either all good or all bad. Her dad and I were all good, and by default, Bill was all bad.

Later we would learn that this type of thinking was a hallmark of borderline personality disorder.

Of course, this wasn't the end of our involvement with CPS. In order to be sure that Lisa had not admitted to lying because she was afraid of us, the CPS worker made another unannounced visit to our home several weeks later. She also talked with the school counselor and with Lisa's teachers. After about two months, she was finally convinced that Lisa had indeed injured herself in hopes of getting rid of her stepfather.

There were no more visits from CPS.

Chapter 23

Ups and Downs

In late February, three months before the end of the school year, Lisa was given an evaluation by the school psychologist, Dr. Margaret Johnson. *At last.*

Dr. Johnson's report was much shorter than Dr. Rios's evaluation, but it largely confirmed what Dr. Rios had observed and recommended. There was one striking and crucial difference, however.

Dr. Johnson, from her interview with Lisa, learned that Lisa feared that she would die and that no one would come to her funeral, feared that others would die, and felt as if she wanted to die sometimes because everyone makes fun of her at school. As a result, Dr. Johnson, in no uncertain terms, stated that Lisa met "the eligibility criteria for a Seriously Emotionally Disturbed Student and is therefore eligible for special education services."

Finally! We had the recommendation we needed.

I felt like the drowning person who had just reached the life preserver.

I was optimistic and confident. I had tried for so long to have Lisa qualified as eligible for special education that it had become somewhat of an obsessive quest to get that small, controlled setting with a certified special education teacher that I hoped would address and solve all her problems. Now we just had to wait for the ARD in three weeks.

It didn't come soon enough. On March 31, five days before the scheduled ARD, I was teaching in class and therefore unreachable by phone. Unable to reach me, Lisa's school called her father. In no uncertain terms, he was told to pick her up from school. Lisa had brought her brother's Swiss Army knife to school and was seen threatening other students with it.

When asked why she had brought the knife to school, she replied that some of the students had been bullying her. The school's zero-tolerance policy for weapons expelled her to the Alternative Learning Center until the ARD in five days.

The Alternative Learning Center was located on a campus about ten miles away. The ALC was basically a "holding tank," and its student population consisted of mostly teenage boys who had been in trouble with the law. Whatever Lisa didn't already know about bad behavior, she learned while she was at the ALC. *While waiting for the stupid ARD.*

At the ARD her behaviors during the past three months were discussed. She had been referred to the principal a total of thirty times, with nineteen tardies, thirteen detentions, nine days in ALC, and one suspension. Dr. Johnson's appraisal was analyzed, and it was finally a done deal. Lisa qualified for a special education program.

Of course it wasn't called that. She was placed into an "adaptive behavior program," with a strict but loving teacher named Mrs. Carl. It was a good match, and the self-contained, single-classroom environment with one nurturing teacher seemed to calm her. Lisa's performance and grades improved dramatically during the final two months of the school year, so she was promoted to seventh grade.

A day or two after the ARD, the Iowa Test of Basic Skills was given to all sixth graders. The results came in during the last week of classes, and they showed that Lisa had scored a grade equivalency of 4.6, putting her in the 16th percentile of all sixth graders in the country.

After wasting almost an entire year with struggles that should have been prevented, she was in the bottom 16% of all sixth graders. She had a grade equivalency of mid-fourth grade, but she was being promoted to seventh? We basically had lost the entire sixth grade while waiting for redundant test results that told us what we already knew anyway.

The successes Lisa enjoyed in the final months of sixth grade carried over into the summer. Since I wasn't teaching summer classes at the college, I was able to devote all of my time to keeping the family stable.

Lisa seemed to be improving, and thus things went better for the entire family. Lisa took swim lessons most of the summer and was becoming quite a fish in the water.

Her successes there, plus the energy she expelled by swimming served to improve her behavior to the extent that we allowed her to attend a one-week YMCA camp at a working ranch in central Texas. She had fun with the various activities such as archery, canoeing, horseback riding, chili cook-offs, and nature adventures.

Still buoyed by her improved behavior, later in the summer, the entire family—Bill, Brian, Lisa, and I—took a family vacation to a Club Med in Huatulco, Mexico. There she excelled at, *of all things*, a one-week circus training program in which she learned to be a performer on the high trapeze.

On the final day of the vacation, the students, including Lisa, put on a circus performance that amazed all the parents. Lisa was fearless and had managed to focus her attention on becoming skilled at this physical and demanding activity.

As a result of her demonstrated skill and interest in acrobatics, when we returned home after the vacation, I enrolled Lisa in a local gymnastics program. She continued to show an interest in the sport and actually became quite proficient for her age.

We attributed much of Lisa's behavioral improvement to her increased self-esteem from her successes in summer activities and in the adaptive behavior program with Mrs. Carl at the end of sixth grade. Seventh grade began hopefully and on the same note with Lisa being assigned once again to the adaptive behavior program.

Suddenly, however, everything fell apart. First, we learned that her dad was moving to Atlanta. This was quite a blow to Lisa because it opened up feelings of abandonment and fear that she wouldn't see her dad as often. Then we were told that Mrs. Carl was no longer her adaptive behavior teacher because she had been reassigned to another classroom.

Predictably, Lisa's school performance began to plummet, and she came home with D's and F's in every subject after six weeks.

In November of seventh grade, yet another ARD was convened to review her deteriorating behavior. Behavioral contracts were drawn up for her to sign in return for allowing her to attend at least one class a day with Mrs. Carl.

Lisa loved her one hour with Mrs. Carl. They had an understanding and rapport similar to the one Lisa had with her Granny. Mrs. Carl was able to identify Lisa's strong points and develop them. For example, Mrs. C. let Lisa help with the deaf and blind students. Lisa was still a champion of the underdog and found self-esteem in helping those with physical disabilities. Mrs. C. called Lisa her "assistant" and told her she could be a good special education teacher some day. Mrs. Carl's weekly reports to us were always positive, and in one, she wrote this about Lisa, "She is an absolute pleasure to me!"

After Christmas, in January, another ARD kept Lisa in the self-contained adaptive behavior program, but with two classes in the mainstream: theatre arts and physical education. She loved both classes and made A's in both of them, with the same comment on her report card by both teachers: "Appropriate behavior." She worked hard as a backstage crew member on the school's spring theatre production entitled "The Boyfriend," and she loved being around the theater and the actors.

Her psychiatrist took her off the Verapamil, so she was now on only three medications, Ritalin, Anafranil, and Imipramine.

In May she failed both the reading and math portions of the TAAS test (Texas Assessment of Academic Skills). On the nationwide Iowa Test of Basic Skills, her results placed her in the 15th percentile of seventh graders nationwide and an equivalent of fifth grade. But she was still promoted to eighth grade.

Chapter 24

Goat Summer

Lisa had many redeeming qualities despite her troublesome behavior. Not the least of these was her compassion for those she thought of as less fortunate, for example, the disabled students in Mrs. Carl's class and the disabled girl she helped on the cruise. She also had a deep love for animals of all kinds.

I had heard about something called Kids 'N Critters summer day camp, which was sponsored by the Humane Animal Welfare Society. Despite the fact that I would be driving sixty miles each way, at 9 a.m. to take her there and at 4 p.m. to pick her up—all in hellish Houston traffic, I signed her up for the weeklong program.

The program focused on animals and their care through activities, games, and arts and crafts. Not only did she learn about animals and their care, but she also had an opportunity to spend time with cats, kittens, dogs, rabbits, guinea pigs, snakes, and many other kinds of animals. She had ample time to cuddle as well as learn about what each type of animal required and what kind of pets they made. Each night at the dinner table, she excitedly shared with us what she had learned that day.

Immediately after Kids 'N Critters camp, she returned to the YMCA ranch camp for the second year. When she came back home, Brian left for the camp to begin his three weeks volunteering as a counselor. It was then that I learned what had transpired during Lisa's week at the camp.

According to Brian, when he arrived and introduced himself to the camp's permanent staff members, they gasped, "Oh, my gosh! Are you Lisa's brother? She has quite a reputation around here!"

When Brian reluctantly responded that he was indeed her brother, they shared why her reputation had preceded him.

One of the activities at the camp was a children's rodeo, and one of the events of the rodeo was goat roping. Goat roping, or goat tying, requires the participant to chase a number of goats in an arena, catch one, throw it down, and tie any three of its legs together.

During Lisa's stay at the camp the week before, she felt that the boys were being unduly rough with the goats and that the event constituted cruelty to animals. She enlisted the help of the other girls at the camp and staged a demonstration demanding that the event be stopped. The senior counselors reluctantly acquiesced and stopped the goat roping event.

Lisa and some of the girls then met with the director of the camp and asked that the goat roping event be eliminated from the rodeo. She was so adamant in her defense of the goats that the director agreed, much to the anger and dismay of the boys in the camp!

Therefore, when Brian arrived, he was met with something less than enthusiasm when the other counselors realized his connection to Lisa.

Chapter 25

Runaway

September of 1996 marked the beginning of the eighth grade for Lisa, and she was again placed in an adaptive behavior class, this time with Mr. Balsam as her teacher. Soon, however, her behaviors became more erratic and frightening. There were five times during the first month of classes that Lisa ran away after school.

The first was during the second week of school. I was waiting for her at the bus stop, but the bus just went on by. I raced to the school, but there was no sign of her. I tracked down the principal and her last-period teacher, who said that Lisa had been in class and had left along with the other students when the final bell rang. But no one knew where she had gone after class.

We called the police to report her missing and were told we had to come to the station to fill out a report. The police officers there were polite and assured us that most kids come back home when they are ready. We returned home, worried sick with no idea if she had run away or if she had been kidnapped.

Finally, after several hours of desperation, around 10 p.m. we heard from her. She called to say she had gone home with a friend after school and was now ready to come home.

Relieved that she was okay, I became angry and asked her why she had not told us where she was going or asked permission. She replied that we probably would not have given permission and she really didn't want to come home anyway, so she decided just to leave.

She told me where she was, and I drove to pick her up at the friend's house. The mom said that she had just gotten home from work and thought Lisa had permission to be there.

We consulted with Lisa's therapist about consequences, and she suggested taking privileges away, which we did. Telephone, television, and computer were forbidden for a week.

I asked her last-period teacher to accompany Lisa to the school bus every afternoon. That worked for a week or two, as Lisa arrived home on time on the bus. One day, however, she did not come home. I phoned the school, and her teacher told me that she had observed Lisa boarding the school bus.

Not knowing what else to do, I contacted the police again and waited. About eight hours later, Lisa finally called around midnight. She said she had indeed gotten on her bus but had gotten off the bus at the home of another student. When we arrived at the friend's home, the mom told us that Lisa had told her that she didn't have any place to go after school because I worked until midnight. Feeling sorry for Lisa, the mom had allowed her to stay the evening.

Yet again a third time in as many weeks, Lisa did not come home, and this time she was gone overnight. She had slipped away from her teacher after school, so no one saw her board the bus, and no one knew where she had gone. I called everyone I could think of and searched all the neighborhoods where I knew her classmates lived. I had accumulated an address book of her friends' names and phone numbers, and I called all of them. No one had seen her.

After a sleepless night of worrying, I finally heard from her the next morning. She called and related that after school the day before, she walked about four miles, crossing a dangerous freeway, to get to Bonnie's house. Bonnie was a friend from school.

When I picked her up, I asked to speak to Bonnie's mother, who said that she didn't even know Lisa was there. I requested of her that if Lisa ever appeared there again, she would call me. She agreed, but I wasn't at all confident of her sobriety at the moment.

I now began picking Lisa up from school myself—at her classroom door. One day as we were walking to the car, she bolted. She began running across the open field adjacent to the school, so I raced after her. Halfway across the field, I stumbled on the uneven ground and fell headlong into the dirt. She turned to look back, saw I had fallen, and she stopped running. Then when she saw that I was getting up and seemed unhurt, she started running again. Embarrassed because half the school had seen me chasing her and falling down, I limped back to my car with hands and knees shaking.

The police sergeant suggested that we enlist the help of the school counselor to see if anything was happening at school to set off these runaway incidents. The counselor told us of an incident in her class the prior week. Lisa was the only girl among eight boys in her adaptive behavior class, so the behavior in that class was rather rowdy, and Mr. Balsam certainly had his hands full.

One day, one of the boys in the class exposed himself to her. She told Mr. Balsam, who promptly called the police. Lisa had to go along to the police station to make a statement. We had not been informed of this incident by the school, nor had Lisa said anything about it.

I don't know if Lisa's experiences in her class had anything to do with her escalating behavior, but I was very frustrated with the school and felt that I couldn't really trust them anymore.

The situation peaked the last weekend in September. Again, Lisa ran away from school when her teacher was distracted while placing another student on a bus. This time, she was missing for the entire weekend.

I don't know how I would have gotten through the weekend without my husband's support, assurances, and encouragement. I don't know how he put up with me. I was, as they say, "worried sick." Anger and fear gnawed at my gut. My head told me she was fine and having a grand old time at some friend's house (which made me angry), but my heart feared for her safety. *What if she was lying dead in a pasture somewhere?* Then there was the gnawing guilt. *What kind of mother was I that my daughter wanted to run away?*

By Monday morning, when she still had not called or returned, I sought the help of the assistant principal. I asked him for the names of all the other students who were absent that day. I pored over the names to see if I recognized any of them. Finally, I identified one girl that I was pretty certain she was with.

I called the school district police and informed them of my suspicions. I asked them to pick Lisa up at that girl's home and charge Lisa with truancy. Privilege withholding had not worked, so it was time for some real-life consequences.

The school police picked her up and took her to the downtown police station, where she was put through the juvenile system. Sometime during the day Lisa was taken to the juvenile detention center, from where I was asked to pick her up at 5 p.m. that same day. She had spent only about five hours there. *Hardly enough time to make an impression of how bad life in juvie would be.*

On the ride home, Lisa was silent. When we arrived home, she got out of the car and went inside. As I was locking all of the doors so she could not escape, her behavior escalated to violence. She picked up a kitchen knife and threw it at me, cutting my leg with a deep two-inch gash.

Then she went into the garage, picked up some garden clippers, and smashed the windshield of Bill's car. She seemed as horrified by her actions as we were but couldn't or wouldn't stop.

Finally, Bill and I were able to grab Lisa and force her into the back seat of my vehicle. She tried to jump out of the moving car as we drove to the nearby hospital emergency room, but we had engaged the child locks on the doors. En route to the hospital, we called her psychiatrist's answering service.

While waiting in the emergency room for the psychiatrist to call back, Lisa calmed down to the point where the emergency personnel wondered why we had brought her there. She was being charming and friendly and showing no signs of belligerence. The emergency room staff shot us looks that suggested Bill and I were the sick ones and she was the victim who needed rescuing from us.

Her psychiatrist Dr. Weaver, however, when told of the day's events, felt Lisa should be admitted to the mental hospital. To her medication he added Depakote, which is used to treat mania in people with bipolar disorder. The next day, October 1, 1996, we took Lisa to be admitted into Shadow Oaks Hospital.

Then came the bombshell. Dr. Weaver told us that he suspects my daughter has a mental condition known as BPD, or borderline personality disorder. He explained that the diagnosis of BPD is usually not given during childhood and adolescence because of the ongoing developmental changes, especially personality. However, since Lisa's manifestations had been consistent throughout childhood and early adolescence, he felt that a diagnosis of BPD might be appropriate, even at her current age of fourteen.

This was a new one for me. I was familiar with the well-known psychiatric diagnoses of schizophrenia, bi-polar disorder, and major depression. *But what was borderline personality disorder and could it be fixed?*

I searched for articles about the diagnosis, but I found very few. It seemed that the disorder had only recently been identi-

fied, and more research and studies needed to be done to understand it more fully. The data that were available indicated that
most psychiatric providers had a negative attitude toward patients with the disorder because BPD patients were often ma-
nipulative, demanding, and prone to rages. Most therapists even
refused to take clients who had been diagnosed with BPD because there was no effective treatment, and they feared the patients wouldn't get any better and might even kill themselves.
Furthermore, there didn't seem to be any consensus on treatment and prognosis was poor.

I was devastated, so I decided not to dwell on this new "fla-
vor of the month" diagnosis. After what I had read, I chose to
hope that this diagnosis was just another stab in the dark by her
psychiatric professionals. After all, she had had numerous diagnoses over the years, including ADHD, fetal alcohol syndrome,
oppositional defiant disorder, attachment disorder, and pervasive
developmental disorder. Whatever what Lisa had was called, we
still had to manage her symptoms and behaviors, which were
growing more and more troubling and more and more dangerous.

She remained an inpatient for about a week before entering
"partial hospitalization," which included a special education program for another two weeks. Dr. Weaver recommended that she
not return to the same environment at her intermediate school
and referred us to a private school.

Lisa was accepted to Memorial Branch Private School for a
trial period during the last week in October; however, after two
days they asked us to withdraw her because of her behavior and
lying. She had apparently alarmed fellow students by telling wild
stories about being raped and beaten and about her brother being in prison for murder.

Her dad, her stepfather, and I (her triumvirate of caregivers)
were overwhelmed and at a total loss about what to do. Her psychiatrist said it was unwise for her to return to public school, yet

we couldn't find an appropriate private school that met her needs. *Or that would accept her.*

Chapter 26

What on Earth Is BPD?

Sometimes the proverbial light bulb goes off in our minds at the strangest time. Our bug exterminator, who also happened to be a longtime friend of Bill's, was kindly listening to us rant about our troubles with Lisa as he walked through our house doing his regular spraying for the ubiquitous Texas pests.

After patiently hearing our complaints and woes, he said something that was so perceptive and insightful that it hit me like a ton of bricks. With gentle concern on his face, he simply said, "Lisa must be in such terrible pain."

I was speechless. Within my own little world of guilt and shame, I had been totally focused on fixing Lisa's behavior. I had never really given much thought to the idea that there might be real inner, emotional pain being expressed outwardly. All I knew was that I had an out-of-control child that I had to figure out how to control if I wanted to consider myself a good parent.

I began to change my frame of mind and attitude from anger and shame to empathy and understanding. A cloud of stress seemed to lift as I tried to grasp what she was feeling inside. She had never been able to describe the feelings that precipitated her behaviors. In later years when she would be trained to identify her feelings, she would describe them as intense, awful, and scary.

I later learned that borderlines have such a weak self-image that they mirror the reactions of others. My anger and shame and guilt were being incorporated into her own self-identity. No one explained this to me then. Therapists didn't know how to treat borderlines; they wouldn't even diagnose it in children or adolescents. Today, early intervention and appropriate counseling have changed all that.

I needed guidance, so I called the Employee Assistance Program associated with my employer, Houston Community College. They helped me set up an appointment in early November with a stern, no-nonsense psychologist who met with Bill and me for two sessions before handing us over to a different therapist.

After listening as we presented, again, our problems with Lisa, the second therapist agreed with the BPD diagnosis. He went on to say, however, that he didn't treat borderlines because they were too demanding and didn't respond to treatment well (a euphemism for "can't be fixed"). He wished us luck in finding a therapist as he ushered us out the door. He added, as we walked away, "Be sure that you don't let her find my phone number."

My husband and I were at a loss as to what to do next. We were angry and frustrated with the mental health community, so I decided that I needed to do some digging myself to find out more about borderline personality disorder. I had never heard of it, and I felt completely incompetent to deal with this diagnosis.

The more I discovered, the more frightened, discouraged, and confused I became.

I learned that the disorder was thought to have both neurotic and psychotic features, hence the term "borderline," and that until 1980 there had been only a dozen research projects published about BPD in the entire world. Some of them proposed theories suggesting that the disorder was the result of failures in early parenting, such as neglect and/or abuse. Other studies blamed over-involved or overprotective parents. Either way, this thought process placed most of the blame on poor mothering. Since the mom was the one most often at home with the child, blame went directly to her. *I was a stay-at-home mom at the time, so was it entirely my fault?*

Fortunately for the guilt-ridden mothers, later studies in the 80's and 90's changed that line of thinking. Biology, specifically genetics, was found to be a major component that seems to predispose certain people to BPD.

Furthermore, there seemed to be a higher incidence of BPD in adopted children, suggesting that the careless behaviors of borderline women often led to unplanned pregnancies. The children born from those pregnancies who were placed for adoption then carried the biological predisposition for developing BPD. *Okay, assuming that it's not all my fault, now what?*

Before we could answer that question, our family received the shocking news that Lisa's beloved Granny, her dad's mother, had died suddenly. Granny was one of the few people who had the ability to "reach" Lisa and to whom Lisa felt really close. Lisa had spent a great deal of time with Granny. Granny was her best friend, and they baked cookies, fed the cattle, did arts and crafts, and gardened together.

I don't know why Lisa responded so well to Granny, but they had a special bond, and Lisa was devastated when Granny died.

It was shortly after Granny's death that Lisa began cutting. At first, we didn't realize what she was doing. When I saw marks on her forearms, she told me they were scratches from the neighbor's cat.

It wasn't until my daughter and I had a confrontation in my kitchen about her being grounded from activities that I personally witnessed her attempt at self-injury.

She grabbed a knife and cut herself on her wrist, bringing blood. I screamed and grabbed the knife out of her hand. At that point, I thought she was just trying to get attention. I would learn later that self-injury was the only way she knew to deal with her emotional pain. It was her coping mechanism.

She admitted to me that she had learned about cutting and how it helped relieve inner pain from other psych patients during group therapy sessions in the hospital. She described one girl who had used nail clippers to slice pieces of skin from her fingers.

With blood streaming down Lisa's arms, she told me that the physical pain is easier to bear than the excruciating emotional pain raging inside. *I just couldn't imagine that kind of pain, but my exterminator had been exactly correct. He had understood it, and I hadn't.*

I was at the end of my rope, feeling exhausted, helpless, and hopeless. There seemed to be no end in sight, and I was terrified because I couldn't help her. I also felt isolated because I couldn't really talk to my friends. My kid was out of control, and theirs weren't. They didn't understand Lisa's problems. *Heck, I didn't understand them.* My own parents' advice was, "Kick her out. MAKE her obey." I felt shame because I had a daughter with these problems, and the old guilt about being a bad parent started creeping in again because nothing I did seemed to make things better.

In desperation, I called Lisa's psychiatrist and told him she had begun cutting. Her psychiatrist, Dr. Weaver, told me that is might be time to call in an educational consultant. An educational consultant is a trained professional who provides private counseling to help students and their families choose appropriate schools based on the students' needs and abilities.

Dr. Weaver put us in touch with one who could see us immediately. His initial consultation would cost $350 for one hour, and his retention fee, if we chose to use his services, would be $1,660. There was no payment plan, the money had to be paid up front, and insurance didn't cover it.

David, Bill, and I met the following day, November 18, 1996, with Dr. Marshall, the consultant, and provided him with all of the psychological reports about Lisa that we had. His opinion was that Lisa's problems were more behavior-oriented than academically-oriented. He believed that Lisa had a non-verbal, social learning disability and didn't understand what was expected of her. As a result, she would become overwhelmed and resort to cutting herself. Self-mutilation was a coping mechanism for her feelings of confusion and hopelessness.

He explained, "Lisa can't organize the social world and how people comport themselves. This frustration leads to the behaviors she exhibits, such as running away, hurting herself, and having raging episodes."

He felt she needed a place that could keep her safe but could teach her socialization skills while addressing her emotional problems. He characterized her as being similar to a feral child, or a child that had been kept in a closet for years.

His plan was three-fold. First, Lisa would attend a therapeutic, behavioral-oriented program, followed by a school that specialized in socialization pragmatics and behavior modification. The last step would be acceptance into a vocational college.

College! Wow! He made it sound so possible. Once again I hoped this would be the magic solution that would help her, even though on some level, I didn't buy into all of it. I wanted to, however, and so I did.

As the first step, Dr. Marshall recommended a 26-day wilderness intervention program in Montana. Wilderness intervention programs are boot camp alternatives with therapy for troubled teens. Dr. Marshall suggested that Lisa be enrolled as soon as possible and made calls to ensure that she could be accepted in the next group that began the next month on January 15, 1997.

I convened our "round table" of three: her dad David, stepfather Bill, and myself. We discussed the continuing downward piral of Lisa's behaviors and agreed that her risk of hurting herself required us to do something fast.

Out of desperation and hopefulness that this therapeutic camp could keep her safe and possibly even turn things around, we agreed to the wilderness program. I had great trepidation, however, about allowing Lisa to do this in the heart of winter in a state with one of the harshest winters in the country.

When we met again with the educational consultant, I mentioned my concerns about the extreme cold. Dr. Marshall assured me that the teens would be spending most of their time in the lodge and would only venture out into the open wilderness if weather permitted. He also gave us a two-page list of references from other educational consultants and families of teens who had gone through the experience with positive results.

I contacted some of the parents listed as references and obtained encouraging feedback. I learned that students are not merely thrown into the wilderness and made to suffer hardships, but that they form bonds with each other, with field staff, and with therapists while they endure adversity and struggle as a group to overcome natural challenges and develop new skills.

It all sounded good. Satisfied that she would be safe, I turned to the cost of the wilderness camp. This was going to be an expensive endeavor.

First, we had to pay upfront the full amount of tuition and fees for the three-week program, which totaled $4,800. Then we had to assemble her clothing and equipment. Required were over a thousand dollars' worth of heavy winter jackets, boots, rain gear, sleeping bag, underwear, hats, and pants. Because we lived in Houston, it was not easy to find the zero-degree-rated items, and we made several trips to REI, Academy, Sun & Ski, and Sears.

Each trip to the store for this extreme winter clothing made me more and more uneasy about the experience. My mother's intuition continued to gnaw at me. My instinctive, emotional reservations about sending her into a Montana wilderness battled with my rational, reasoning trust in her doctors, who agreed that this was what she needed. The rational won out, but I would soon learn never to ignore my mother's intuition.

Because the enormous expense of the wilderness program came just before Christmas, we decided to give Lisa some of the wilderness clothing as Christmas presents, such as the attractive fleece jacket and a cute hat and matching gloves.

Lisa, however, was not at all happy about her gifts and spent the entire Christmas Day complaining and pouting and crying about not having gotten anything that SHE wanted. *What? After all the money we spent on her?*

I didn't know how to feel or to react. My knee-jerk response was to be infuriated by her selfishness in the wake of our spending thousands of dollars for the upcoming camp.

On the other hand, I understood that this horrible affliction that she had been given was no picnic for her either. After all, one significant symptom of borderline personality disorder was the inability to manage emotions. She must have been pretty scared about going so far away, not to mention the confusion about why she was different from the other kids.

Chapter 27

What's Frostbite?

L isa spent a week with her dad in Atlanta the first week in
January, and soon after returning, it was time to put her on a
plane for Spokane, Washington, where she would be met by
staff of the wilderness program and transported by car to the
Trout River Wilderness Camp in the mountains of northwest
Montana.

I was told that we would not be in contact with Lisa or anyone from the camp for eleven days, at which time one of the
therapists would initiate a phone conference.

We never got that far. On Saturday, January 25, just ten days
into the wilderness evaluation, I received a call from one of the
therapists that had been with Lisa in the wilderness. She told me
that Lisa was in a hospital in Great Falls, Montana, with severe
frostbite on her fingers and her feet. I got on the earliest plane
for Great Falls, which left the next morning at 8 a.m.

I grew up in the South, so frostbite was a condition I knew
nothing about. I was aware that the term had always been used
loosely to refer to very cold fingers and toes, but I had never
known anyone who had suffered from actual frostbite in the
medical sense. I had absolutely no appreciation for the serious-

94

ness of the condition and no hint of what I would see when I got to the hospital.

When I arrived at the Great Falls airport, the director of the wilderness camp met me and drove me to the hospital, all the way assuring me that the camp was not in any way responsible for what had happened and that Lisa would be fine. She stressed the round-the-clock presence at Lisa's side by staff members since my daughter arrived at the hospital.

I'll never forget what I saw when I entered my daughter's hospital room. The sight was completely and unexpectedly horrifying. Her legs were stiff and swollen to at least twice their size with bluish-black, blood-filled blisters on every area of her feet. Loose, sterile gauze separated the toes, which looked like black golf balls. Her fingers were stiff, hard, and wooden-looking, and they had the texture of a frozen piece of chicken. The tips of her swollen fingers were turning hard, black, and blistered as they re-warmed and filled with blood.

My horror turned to nausea as the nurse informed me that Lisa had advanced frostbite on her legs and hands and that her condition was extremely serious. She explained that in deep frostbite, the muscles, tendons, blood vessels, and nerves all freeze, and use of the area is lost, sometimes temporarily and sometimes permanently. Nerve damage in the area can result in a loss of feeling, tissue death, and subsequent amputation if gangrene or infection sets in.

The nurses had made pen marks on her legs, marking the distance from her feet where she still had sensation. Prick tests had been done every hour, and the distance that the numbness was progressing up the leg (or as they referred to it, the anesthetic area) was increasing every time it was measured. She currently had feeling in her legs to just below the knees. There was no sensation in either leg below that.

She was experiencing significant pain as the areas were warmed and blood flow established. What had begun as a dull continuous ache transformed into an extremely painful throbbing sensation. She was being given large doses of pain medication, plus antibiotics and anti-inflammatories. I was told that the prognosis was poor for her type of injury and to brace myself for the possibility of amputations.

I was still in shock, so I barely heard the nurse when she added, "Of course, Lisa's youth is an encouraging factor, as young people are more likely to regenerate and recover than older people." All I heard in my brain was, "Cut off her fingers and feet," running on a continuous loop.

Several times during the next hour, staff came in and took multiple photographs of her extremities. They said that in all their years of living in Montana, they had never seen a more extreme case of frostbite.

A few hours after I arrived, a uniformed, armed officer of the law came into the room. He introduced himself as the sheriff of Glacier County, Montana, and told us that he was collecting evidence to determine if child endangerment and abuse charges should be filed against the wilderness camp.

He informed us that the temperature had been twenty degrees below zero the night Lisa contracted frostbite, with a wind chill of forty below. He said that the teens were subjected to an extreme health hazard and had no ability to survive in such cold temperatures.

He added that sheriff deputies had found the campsite and determined that it was located in an avalanche zone. Furthermore, some of the counselors had been skiing above the snow caves where the group slept, thus adding to the instability and danger. The deputies evacuated the area and sent the remaining campers, staff, and therapists back to the home-base lodge. The wilderness experience was over for this group.

As Lisa told the story of her experience to the officer, it was the first time I heard in her own words what had happened:

"We spent the first four days hiking long distances in the mountains and camping in the evenings under canvas that was stretched across rope or in snow caves that we ourselves built into snow banks or snowdrifts.

On the fourth night, one of the teens ran away, and after the staff searched for a long time, she was found and returned to the camp. As a result, to prevent anyone else from running away, the camp counselors took away our boots, and we had to sleep in our socks. I asked them if I could keep my boots because I have a bladder problem and have to go to the bathroom several times a night. They refused, so when I had to pee in the middle of the night, I walked out into the snow in my socks and peed.

I crawled back into my sleeping bag after putting on dry socks, but some of the moisture from the snow must have stayed on my feet because the socks became wet. I didn't have another pair of dry socks because we were only allowed to have two pairs with us.

When the counselors returned our boots to us the next morning, I put my boots on and joined the group for our morning hike. In the evening when we were told to take our boots off, I couldn't get mine off because my feet were frozen and swollen, and I couldn't feel anything.

The counselors said they were not allowed to start a fire, so they rubbed some fire paste on my boots, and lighted it to warm my boots enough that they could get them off my feet. When they saw my white, stiff feet and toes, the staff immediately began tearing off their jackets and shirts and wrapped them around my feet to keep them warm. They also removed my gloves, which were stuck to my fingers, and wrapped my hands. Then they wrapped my entire body with jackets and blankets.

A male staff member and one of the teens made a stretcher out of some limbs and carried me about three or four miles through the woods to an isolated road, where they flagged down some Blackfeet Native Americans in a pickup truck.

They took us to the Blackfeet Indian Hospital on their reservation in Browning, Montana, which is near Glacier National Park. I was seen right away by a doctor, who said that my frostbite was too severe for him to treat and that I needed to be taken right away to the nearest major hospital, which was in Great Falls, about three hours away by car. The ambulance got there in less than two hours."

The sheriff took copious notes as Lisa spoke. After she completed her story, the sheriff took photographs of her feet and hands and gathered contact information from us. The sheriff said they would likely try to shut the camp down and would be contacting us to testify.

I stayed the night in the hospital room with my daughter and anxiously awaited each visit by the nurse who did a prick test to monitor the extent of Lisa's numbness. Finally, the next morning, the numbing that had been silently, surreptitiously creeping up her legs reversed direction. Feeling was beginning to return to her legs just below the knee. Subsequent prick tests during the day demonstrated increasing sensation returning.

As the feeling in her legs returned, her pain was suffocating, and she was constantly monitored by a pain team, who dispensed morphine as needed.

The fact that her sense of touch was coming back was joyful news, but the dark, bluish black, swollen discoloration was getting worse. Her feet looked like bulging circus-clown shoes, with the black discoloration covering all of both feet. The fingers were also turning black and cyanotic from the first knuckles to the tips, which looked like purplish-black chicken drumsticks.

The threats of gangrene, infection, and possible amputation were still present, and she remained in considerable pain. Pediatricians, orthopedists, plastic surgeons, dermatologists, pain specialists, and various other hospital personnel continued to stream into the room to snap photos throughout the day. Although still highly sedated, Lisa seemed to thrive on being the focus of so much attention. *I don't think she ever comprehended the seriousness of her situation.*

Although I had my camera with me, for some reason, I did not take a single photo. The entire scenario was still surreal, and I was in emotional shock from the sudden, unexpected fear and stress. I felt dazed, numb, and detached, as if I were witnessing something from outside my body. This still-unfolding horror story was too painful to document with photos, and I was too worried even to think of taking a photo.

I also felt responsible for making the decision that put her in this situation and wanted nothing to remind me of my guilt.

Days later, when anger replaced the daze, I resented those photo hounds for treating Lisa like a circus freak. I was furious with the wilderness camp counselors for allowing this to happen. I was also furious with myself. *Why didn't I trust my instincts? I guess I was just so desperate to find that magic pill which would help her. I asked myself, "If amputation is necessary, will we have monumental physical challenges in addition to the mental challenges we already have?" In my mind the future had become imponderable.*

Chapter 28

The Ten Little Piggies Stayed Home

After three days in the Montana hospital, Lisa was released and referred to a plastic surgeon back in Houston, who would monitor her progress. He told us that he had only seen two or three cases of frostbite in his many years of practice in Houston and that those were simple cases of frostbitten noses received while skiing on vacation.

Needless to say, this Houston plastic surgeon, like all the doctors before him, took many photographs of Lisa, documenting her condition. He said it was a once-in-a-lifetime chance to document such a severe case and asked me to sign a release giving him permission to use the photos in a medical textbook.

Although the danger of amputation of any of her limbs was no longer a threat because of Lisa's quick response to antibiotics and her "youthful resilience," the need for skin grafts was a distinct possibility in the future. Everything depended on the extent of tissue loss and the extent of healing that would occur over the next few months. No one could gauge the outcome of her feet and hands, what would be left, and how they were to look for the rest of her life. But at least she would be able to keep all of her fingers and toes.

Lisa spent the month of February at home recuperating. She was still taking antibiotics to prevent infection, and I performed strict sterile dressing changes twice daily. The removed dressings looked vile and nasty. Flesh chunks, looking as if they had been gnawed away by rats, were missing from her feet and fingers. The sight always left me feeling nauseated, depressed, and anxious.

I spoke to her doctor frequently, and he continued to encourage us, saying that her age was a powerful factor in her favor for a miraculous recovery. "Kids have incredible healing ability," he would often tell us.

Finally, around day thirty, her wounds stopped oozing and bandages were no longer necessary. Slowly, over a period of several weeks, we watched the blackened shells around her feet and the blackened "mushroom caps" at the end of her fingers fall off, revealing deformed, but pink and shiny skin. She couldn't seem to resist scratching the often intense itching she felt, but the skin was so sensitive and fragile that scratching was agonizing. She had lost all of her toenails and most of her fingernails, but it looked as if major skin grafting would not be necessary except on the most serious areas of her toes and fingers.

Very slowly, most of her fingernails began to grow back, but the fingers remained very stiff. The freezing had gone deep into the bone, so she still had no feeling in her big toes, and pain made walking difficult. She described the sensation in her toes as "feeling like they're ready to snap off." It would be a long recovery.

In the meantime, I had received several phone calls from Montana (sheriff's office, insurance company, etc.), asking for releases of information about Lisa's injuries. The sheriff's office informed me that, after their investigation, felony charges were indeed being brought against the wilderness camp for child endangerment and abuse. The county attorney called to say that his office was also prosecuting the two camp guides for negligence.Still traumatized from the entire episode, I hoped I would not have to participate in any testimony or legal action. I was assured by the county attorney that they had enough evidence without needing my or Lisa's testimony.

Because Lisa's hospitalization and doctor visits were covered by my medical insurance, the only extra expense we incurred because of the frostbite was the cost of airfare and of course, the cost of the aborted wilderness assessment.

I sent my airplane ticket receipt to the wilderness camp director, asking for reimbursement for my flight as well as for the approximately $5,000 I had paid for the wilderness course and associated fees.

I received a curt response about a month later and a check in the amount of $2,700. They did not reimburse me for the airfare, and they deducted the following from the $5,000 I had paid: prorated fee for 10 days of the course that she completed, as well as $170 per day for individual care (staying with her in the hospital until I arrived), and an "escort" fee of $100, presumably for picking me up from the airport. *Seriously? A hundred bucks to take me eight miles from the airport to my daughter's hospital room where she was suffering because of THEM! A taxi would have been cheaper.*

I wanted to forget everything about Montana and the wilderness camp, so I just accepted the check and let the money issue drop. I never found out the result of the sheriff's case against them, but according to the camp's website, they are still in business. However, their wilderness camps are now only held during the months of June, July, and August.

At least there won't be any more frostbite cases.

Chapter 29

Dad Tries It for a Week

As soon as Lisa was able to walk and hold a pencil, she returned to her public middle school in eighth grade for several weeks in March while continuing to heal. In the meantime, we continued seeing Dr. Weaver, who added the medications Adderall and Depakote to the Anafranil and Ritalin she
was already taking.

My spring break from teaching at the college did not corre-
spond to Brian and Lisa's spring break, so Lisa's dad agreed to
fly down from Atlanta and care for them while Bill and I took a
much-needed vacation trip.

Here is David's account of what happened while we were
gone:

"I took Lisa to school the morning of Friday, March 7, and
met one of her teachers. Then the three of us (Brian, Lisa, and I)
spent the entire weekend at the family farm. Everything went
okay during the weekend. Monday also went okay, but then on
Tuesday the school diagnostician called me and said that Lisa
had not taken her morning medication that day. She also said
that I really should be ashamed of myself for not being as good
on ensuring that Lisa took her medication as her mother did.

My notes say that I saw Lisa take a pill that morning, take a drink of liquid, and then open her mouth to confirm that nothing was left. The lady said that Lisa had been using bad language all morning. The nurse was not there to administer Lisa's noon medication, so I had to bring it to her.

On Wednesday Lisa had asked for her multiplication chart to take a test. She was denied her chart and told to do the work herself. A student named Mark was allowed to have his multiplication chart, so Lisa pulled a fit. I was called to pick her up early from school that day. Her regular teacher, Mr. Balsam, was not there that day, and she had a substitute.

On Thursday Lisa had been taking the bandages off her feet and showing her black, peeling, frostbitten toes to the class. It was making everybody sick. I was again called to pick her up and was talking to her adaptive-behavior teacher, Mr. Balsam. I meant to reassure him by placing a friendly hand on his shoulder. He backed away quickly and wouldn't let me near him. It seems that one of the other parents had clobbered him on his face.

On Friday we had an appointment with her frostbite doctor, so she was out of school for half a day. Thank goodness you will be back tomorrow."

One week and he had enough. The other fifty-one weeks were now mine again.

I was still faced with finding an appropriate school setting for my daughter because public school just wasn't addressing her needs, behaviorally or academically. On numerous occasions Bill or I had to pick up Lisa from school early because of her behavior. Once she kicked a hole in the wall, and another time she hid Mr. Balsam's phone from him.

We again conferred with the educational consultant, Dr. Marshall, who suggested therapeutic boarding school. "Lisa's history of disregard for family rules, violent and often destructive behavior, difficulty managing anger, and manipulation of situations to escape consequences make her a prime candidate for a therapeutic boarding school," he said.

The consultant explained that these schools are private educational institutions for troubled teens with trained professional staff, a structured learning environment with constant supervision, and small classes. He cautioned us that they were expensive, but that they have worked miracles with students with their one-on-one therapeutic interventions.

The other alternatives he mentioned were the more intense residential treatment option (sort of a hospital-jail) and boot camp. We decided to try the least intense option, the therapeutic boarding school.

Dr. Marshall called the Creek Ranch School, located several hours outside of Santa Fe, New Mexico, to find out if they would accept Lisa. He explained to the headmaster that Lisa was an anxious, impulsive child with a history of stealing. In addition, he said that she lacked self-management and has been explosive. He forwarded copies of Lisa's previous psychological testing.

The headmaster, after conferring with other school staff members, told Dr. Marshall that an interview would be needed before they could say for certain if she would be accepted. Until they could talk to Lisa face-to-face, there were no guarantees. She was academically compatible, but her emotional issues would have to be addressed at the interview.

On March 20, 1997, Lisa and I flew to Santa Fe to be interviewed for placement in Creek Ranch School. Creek Ranch was highly recommended for its behaviorally-oriented, therapeutic program in a rural setting, allowing students to explore nature and work with animals such as horses, rabbits, and dogs. Because of Lisa's great love for animals, she was very excited about the prospect of attending this school.

Upon arriving in Santa Fe, I rented a car, and Lisa and I drove about thirty miles in the beautiful pine-covered New Mexico Mountains to the Creek Ranch Campus, a former 300-acre dude ranch. The setting was picture-book rustic, with buildings made of logs, trout ponds, barns, and stables. Both Lisa and I were in awe of the beautiful surroundings, and of course, she immediately zeroed in on the horses and dogs that greeted us. As far as she was concerned, this place was perfect.

Lisa was interviewed by staff, and the interview went well, of course. Lisa can muster up her best behavior and really turn on the charm when she wants something.

The notes from the interview were laudatory. One staff member said:

"Lisa presents well—good eye contact—articulate. Wants to be here. Quizzed her about bed-wetting. She says under control with medication. Should developmentally take care of itself. Good report card. I like this girl, think we should take her ASAP. Get her out of the school she's in."

Another said:

"Nice, sweet kid. Good interview. Would fit into the student body somewhere in the middle. Mom seems supportive. Lisa is worried about being away from her mom. We discussed a telephone policy. She will need extra support in the beginning to adjust and make the separation from the mother."

After the interview, I spoke with the director and expressed concern that, according to their brochure, they accepted "emotionally sound students who are classified as learning disabled or who need a little more guidance than a public school can provide." I expressed my doubts that Lisa could be considered emotionally sound.

The director assured me that after interviewing Lisa, she felt that Lisa was sufficiently emotionally stable to succeed at Creek Ranch School and that their specialized teachers could help her build confidence in herself.

I wanted desperately to believe it, so I did.

After the discussion with the director, Lisa and I were taken on a tour of the ranch, which housed sixty students and thirty staff members. The dormitories were all log cabins with fireplaces in the living rooms. The vocational and recreational facilities included computer labs; an art shed for sculpting, painting, and throwing pots; a photo lab for developing pictures; a stable, barn, and riding ring where students not only ride horses but also maintain tack, groom, and care for horses (I thought I'd never get Lisa out of there!); tennis, basketball, and volleyball courts; baseball and soccer fields; and ponds for fishing and ice skating.

It was perfect. It was idyllic. And Lisa was enthralled. I began to really believe that this was the place that would help Lisa develop her potential. I had to believe it—especially when I wrote an eight-thousand-dollar check for the remaining two months of the school year.

We flew back home to assemble her clothes and supplies so that she could begin classes immediately. The list of required items was nowhere near as long or as expensive as the one for the wilderness camp had been. In fact, the necessities were routine, and she already owned everything she would need except for a pair of leather work gloves and a riding helmet. *This was good news after writing the check for eight thousand dollars.*

With three suitcases, Lisa flew back to New Mexico three days after our visit. We called her about once a week for the first few weeks. Communication with parents during the first couple of weeks was usually discouraged to allow the student to adjust to the boarding school environment. Even after that, parents and students were encouraged to communicate by mail rather than telephone. In Lisa's case, however, an exception was made because of her separation anxiety from me.

About two weeks after Lisa arrived at the school, I received a call from a staff member about Lisa's progress. Among the positive points he mentioned: "Lisa is fitting in well with the program. She has already bonded with several students. She is adjusting to the rules at the school, but she is very, very hyperactive."

Lisa's first letter to us came at about the same time, just before Easter.

"Dear Mom,

Hi, how are you doing? I'm doing just fine. I love it up here. Everybody is really nice to me. I have made a lot of nice friends. I am having a lot of fun. I had over 90 points for three days in a row, so I am on level 3. It means I can stay up late one night a week and I can go on a field (sic) trip to Santa Fe. My vocational electives are journlism (sic) and equine management. My favorite horse is Stubby. How is the family? Well, I have nothing more to say exept (sic) I love you and I want you to wright (sic) me back.

P.S. Happy Easter

Love, Lisa"

Gradually, as the first few weeks went on, my feelings of anxiety and concern were being replaced by real hope that this school was the right fit for my daughter and that it would prove to be the answer to our prayers. *Could this school actually be the one to help her?*

Chapter 30

A River Runs through It

W e had about a month of these rose-colored feelings before the call came from a school administrator in early May.

Lisa had lost two levels of privileges after using curse words to a staff member. In addition, she had been telling lies about how she had been raped the previous summer. The administrator told us that Lisa had recently broken up with her boyfriend there at the school, and probably as a result, was exhibiting attention-seeking behavior.

Two days later on May 9, another call came, this time from the school nurse, who reported that Lisa was trying to hurt herself. The nurse said that Lisa's behavior often becomes unmanageable after 8 p.m., when she is often out of control, using severe curse words and "sailor language" with wild behavior and rage. Most recently, when they put her in isolation, she dug her fingernails into her arms, making bloody lacerations. When she was asked why she did it, she said she was angry.

The nurse continued, "Lisa didn't know how to express her anger, so she tried to hurt herself to relieve her feelings of angerand rage. She doesn't know what to do about anger, so she goes berserk."

The nurse suggested that Lisa needs to learn to recognize when she is out of control and ask for a time out or scream—some acceptable form of behavior, not scratching her arms—to get rid of her anger, and that this is a skill that Lisa will need to work on over and over. She also mentioned that perhaps the dosages of Adderall and Depakote needed to be increased for anger management.

I received no more phone calls until the end of school, so I assumed the increased dosages of her medication had helped.

End-of-semester activities and awards were scheduled for May 23, and parents were invited. Unfortunately, Lisa's brother, Brian, was graduating from our local high school the same day, so we did not attend the festivities in New Mexico.

I felt guilty, but I couldn't be in two places at the same time. It wasn't until a week later, through the mail, that I learned that Lisa had received several eighth-grade awards. They were "recognition for outstanding endeavor" in U.S. history, journalism, fitness, and horsemanship. I really felt bad then because I hadn't been there to show my pride in her accomplishments. *I couldn't be in two places at once.*

The results of the Test of Basic Skills, which was a school-normed evaluation, also came in the mail, reporting that all of her quarterly grades were passing. Her grade equivalency was shown to be at ninth grade in language, except for spelling, which was at a sixth grade level. Math was at a seventh grade level.

I was greatly encouraged by the awards and her grades, and I actually looked forward to her coming home for the summer in a few days and then returning to Creek Ranch in September.

After a couple of weeks at home during which Lisa reconnected with some of her friends, in early June she and her brother flew to Atlanta to spend a couple of weeks with their dad. When they returned, things were still looking bright. I was confident we were on the right track with this school and began planning for her next semester there for the first year of high school!

Then I got a call from the headmaster of Creek Ranch.

The headmaster informed me that Lisa's return to Creek Ranch next term was tentative. I was stunned, of course, and bewildered. I told him that no one on the staff had called us since we had increased her medication, and I had thus assumed that all was well.

The headmaster proceeded to inform me about what he called a serious incident that had occurred during the last week of classes. He said that Lisa had pushed a girl, Emily, into the river that flows through the camp. The river was flooding, and it took at least ten minutes to rescue Emily from the dangerous waters.

In an incident report, which I received later, Emily described in detail how the incident occurred:

"Lisa and I were walking by the river behind the cabin. Lisa told me to see how cold the water was. I said no. Lisa then asked, 'Why? Do you think I'll push you in? I wouldn't do that to my best friend.' So I went and checked the water with my hand. Then Lisa ran up and pushes me in the water. I was up to my chin and I was struggling to get out for a long time. I asked her to help me, but she ran off laughing toward the tennis courts."

The headmaster went on to tell us that "this was just one of several episodes the past month." He said that he himself was doubtful about Lisa's return next term, but that her teachers' opinions are split and there is no consensus. He expressed doubts about her stability and felt that a more therapeutic environment would be better. He agreed to call us again in a week after the entire staff had met.

This repetition of the term "therapeutic environment" was beginning to grate on me just as the constant repetition of "falling through the cracks" *had become a mantra in elementary school. All of the schools we looked at called themselves "therapeutic." What do they mean by <u>more</u> therapeutic?*

The next week the headmaster phoned. His voice was apologetic as he gave me the camp's decision that Lisa was not invited back. "Her primary issue is one of safety," he said.

"Lisa needs a setting where she can't get into trouble—a closer environment with closer supervision, a smaller campus. Perhaps not a locked facility but a place where there is someone to help her reign in her impulses when she can't."

*Isn't that what the school had said that **they could do**? Again, as with the wilderness camp, Lisa had proved to be more than they could or would handle. I was beginning to understand what "more therapeutic" meant. It meant "more supervision" and thus, "more money."*

He concluded with a somewhat optimistic comment that suggested she might be allowed to come back some day: "When she comes back, we want her to be safe. Her task is to control her impulses."

In the school record of communication, he wrote:

"Called Lisa's mom and had a candid discussion. Lisa is not currently appropriate for Creek Ranch School as she has the potential for harm to self and others. Mom understands and is supportive. She appreciates our hard work and notes that Creek Ranch is the first school about which Lisa was happy. I said we would hold open the possibility of her return following several months of stability. Mom is working with educational consultant Dr. Marshall."

Well, here it was. Another kick in the teeth. Now what? Back to square one.

Fortunately, Lisa was at a friend's house during and after the conversation, so I just lay my head on the kitchen table and cried. I cried for Lisa, and I cried for myself. I cried because I didn't know what else to do.

I dreaded telling Lisa because I knew she was looking forward to returning to the school, and I knew it would be another rejection that she would have difficulty handling. I was afraid she wouldn't know how to handle it and would act out. My trepidations would later be proved correct. It was going to be a summer like no other.

Chapter 31

The First Summer from Hell

I wanted to have a plan before telling Lisa she was not going back to Creek Ranch for school in September, so in a few days I called Creek Ranch's headmaster for advice. We discussed in more detail the type of environment he felt she needed. It was an honest discussion, and he straightforwardly told me that Lisa needed an environment where she would be watched twenty-four hours a day with behavioral counseling on a specialized basis. He knew of three such schools in Pennsylvania, Connecticut, and Colorado. Each one cost between $60,000 and $75,000 per year.

I knew that it would take the rest of the summer to decide on a plan, so I decided to go ahead and tell Lisa of Creek Ranch's decision. Predictably, she was devastated. She was stunned at first and then her eyes welled up with tears. She ran up to her room and closed the door. I tried to follow her, but she said she wanted to be alone. I insisted that she keep her door open at least a sliver, so I could be sure she was okay.

To her, this was a rejection of major proportions. I felt really bad about the situation, too, and I didn't have a clue about how to soften the blow. I heard her on the phone, talking with friends, so I went into the kitchen to begin preparing dinner. An hour or so later, I called upstairs to tell Lisa that dinner was ready. There was no answer. I bounded up the stairs to find her bedroom window open. She had apparently climbed out of the upstairs window and jumped from it. She was nowhere to be found.

I immediately located Bill and her brother, Brian, and we began looking for her and calling her friends. No one knew anything. We were frantic. I didn't sleep all night, fearing for her safety. She didn't call us to say she was okay as she often did when she ran away, so I had no idea if she was safe or dead.

Early the next morning, we finally received a phone call. The caller was a man who identified himself and said that he had just discovered my daughter sleeping under his sixteen-year-old son's bed. He said that we should come and get her right away because her legs were swollen to the size of tree trunks.

He gave us his address, which was across Houston, about an hour away. When Bill and I arrived at the modest, middle-class home in a working-class section of the city, Lisa was in a lot of pain and unable to walk. Both legs indeed looked like tree trunks, swollen and discolored.

Bill carried her to our car and drove at once to the emergency room at a hospital near our home. En route, Lisa unwillingly told us what happened.

The day before, when she was in her room after being told of Creek Ranch's decision, she called the boyfriend (who could drive) of one of her friends and asked him to come and get her. She watched from her window until she saw him drive up to our neighbor's house, where he waited for her.

Lisa jumped out of her second-story bedroom window, landing with, as she later put it, "a loud crack in both legs." She said she couldn't walk, so she crawled on her hands and knees about half a block to where the boy was parked in his pick-up truck. He then drove her to his house and she hid under his bed all night, in terrible pain.

I guess the boy got scared and told his father the next morning, and he immediately called us.

The emergency room doctor took x-rays of Lisa's legs and referred us without delay to an orthopedic surgeon. Both legs were fractured at the ankle, and she would need surgery because joints were involved. Since this was Friday afternoon, the surgery would be the following Monday morning at 7 a.m.

Lisa's ankles were realigned with plates and screws, and she was placed in two casts that went from her toes to the bottoms of her knees. She was released to home late in the evening on the same day and told to keep her weight off her legs for six weeks.

She was also supposed to be confined to a wheelchair for a week, but by the next day she was walking around with casts on both legs, stiff-legged, like a robot. She even maneuvered the stairs in her casts.

Three days later, we had another visit to the emergency room when Lisa announced from the top of the stairs that her glass of water had shattered and she thought she had swallowed some glass. We loaded her into the car, complete with casts and wheelchair.

Hours later, we were told that glass wouldn't show up on an x-ray, but since there had been no vomiting or coughing blood, the glass had probably passed through the esophagus and stomach. They informed us that there was nothing to worry about because the bowel is able to handle even sharp shards of glass and there is rarely a perforation. We were told to "wait and see" and come back if there were any unusual symptoms, such as acute pain, that might indicate a complication.

The summer that had started so promisingly with hopes of returning to Creek Ranch School had taken a sharp turn in the opposite direction the very day Lisa found out that she would not be returning.

Fortunately, her frostbitten hands and feet had healed miraculously. She still had no feeling in the tips of her fingers or in her big toes, but the new skin had grown in nicely and skin grafts would not be required. She would always have some minor disfiguration of her fingertips and toe tips, but she had been extremely lucky. Her youth had indeed worked to her favor in healing what all the experts regarded as potentially life-threatening injuries.

Chapter 32

Father Knows Best

Lisa's dad, who now lived in Atlanta, decided at this point that he was going to take over her behavior management.

David took a month of medical leave from his job, drove from his home in Atlanta to Houston to pick her up, and announced that she would be staying with him for at least a month.

In the meantime, he was going to have her seen by professionals in the Atlanta area. He seemed confident that he could turn Lisa's behavior around with a little stern fathering.

As her dad drove away with Lisa and her broken legs stretched across the back seat, I began to sob quietly. Bill turned to me and said, "You know, I really and truly hope that living with her dad will be the magic pill for Lisa; yet part of me hopes that she gives him the same hell that she has been giving us, so he sees what we've been going through."

It was such an honest admission of his feelings that I started laughing hysterically. Soon he joined me, laughing and crying at the same time right there on the front lawn of our home. It was as if her leaving with David had allowed our emotions of frustration, anxiety, and helplessness to surface and erupt.

It only took a few days after her arrival in Georgia for Lisa to initiate her father in the fine art of her behavior issues. Their first visit to the emergency room involved Lisa getting a bone stuck in her throat while her dad was barbecuing. David tried to assure her that she was okay, but according to him, she started having a panic attack, so he drove her to the emergency room, where the doctors assured her that she was fine.

After that, there was some type of emergency every night. She would get something in her eye, be sunburned, fall and bump her head, have a rash, "accidentally" cut herself, etc. Finally, after about a week of this, there was a real emergency.

David, at Lisa's urging, had bought a kitten. After the two of them took the kitten to the veterinarian for its shots, Lisa went into her bedroom with the kitten. Before going into her bedroom, she filled a five-ounce Solo cup with Isopropyl alcohol, stating that she was going to wash the area where the cat received the shot.

Later that evening, David took her medication, Anafranil and Depakote, to her in her upstairs bedroom. Lisa reached over and grabbed the cup of liquid on her bed table and swallowed her pills. After about two gulps, she commented to her dad that she believed that what she was drinking was not water. She also stated her throat and stomach burned, and in the process remembered she had poured alcohol into the cup.

David called 911, and Lisa was transported to the nearest hospital by ambulance.

David explained to the doctors that he believed the ingestion was accidental, but that Lisa seems to "set up accidents to happen." The doctors recommended therapy, and David informed them that Lisa had already begun seeing a therapist since coming to Georgia and would continue to do so.

In the emergency room, a saline gastric lavage was done and charcoal was administered. She was admitted overnight and hydrated throughout the night. She insisted that the ingestion was accidental, and since all the toxicology screens were negative, she was sent home the next morning.

Another emergency room visit occurred a few days later, following Lisa's ingestion of a bottle of cough syrup. This time she did it deliberately, telling the admitting physician, "I tried to commit suicide because my life sucks."

She was admitted to the psychiatric unit of the hospital and the next morning received a psychiatric evaluation.

The doctor's report stated the following: "Patient states that she has been depressed for the last three or four years and has felt suicidal about that long. She says she cut herself on her arms and face at least twelve times because when she sees the blood come out, she feels relief and no longer feels depressed. She states that she has trouble sleeping because her stepfather beats her about twice a week."

When David informed me about what had happened and told me what Lisa had said about Bill beating her, I was angry and disappointed but not surprised since she had made that accusation before. She now had a new audience who didn't know her history of lying and had obviously decided to try that stunt again.

Unfortunately, her father was not convinced that Lisa was lying about Bill beating her, and this made me furious. I angrily replied, "You can choose to believe her instead of me, but one of these days she is going to lie about you, and then you'll learn firsthand what she is capable of." Then we hung up on each other.

The hospital psychiatrist's diagnosis did little to illuminate Lisa's issues. He simply diagnosed her as having major depression and ADHD and recommended continued psychiatric treatment. *No blockbuster news here.*

After four days in the hospital's psych unit, she was considered stabilized and was released.

While Lisa was still in the hospital, David enlisted the help of another educational consultant. David had never liked Dr. Marshall in Houston and said that now since Lisa was in Georgia, he wanted his own consultant who would search for appropriate school placements for Lisa.

A day or so after her release, David took Lisa to an educational consultant in Atlanta for yet another psychological evaluation. He faxed me the report, which told us little that we had not already learned from her four previous appraisals. Her IQ tested about the same, at 89, which was low average, and she was identified as learning disabled in math.

However, this psychologist was the first to address in detail Lisa's propensity for self-mutilating behavior. She stated that Lisa would rather hurt on the outside (physically) by cutting herself than hurt on the inside (emotionally) with the depression and the pain of strong feelings that seem too difficult to bear.

She went on to say in her report that Lisa always regrets the act of cutting but cannot control the impulse. She correctly theorized that Lisa had probably learned about cutting from disturbed peers at her schools.

The therapist added that many people who self-mutilate do not feel any physical pain when they are hurting themselves because the emotional pain causes the brain to release opiate-like chemicals that act as a kind of pain reliever. Unfortunately, these self-harming behaviors can become addictive when a person begins to crave that rush of opiates and their calming effect. She warned that once someone starts cutting, it can be hard to stop.

The psychologist's diagnosis was a complex one:

Axis I (clinical syndromes): major depression, ADHD, math learning disability, oppositional defiant disorder with self mutilating risk

Axis II (personality disorders & mental retardation): rule out borderline personality disorder. *Rule out means "suspected."*

Axis III (physical disorders): recently broke both ankles

Axis IV (environmental and psychosocial stressors): death of grandmother, divorced parents, father moving to Georgia, poor choice of friends, educational problems

Axis V (highest level of functioning during past year): 48%

Recommendations: an educational environment that offers supervision.

In other words, "therapeutic."

One month after "taking charge of Lisa," David was feeling the frustration of dealing with her issues. Then came the final straw—the one I had warned him about.

Lisa had met a boy named Shawn at Creek Ranch School. Shawn lived in California, and he and Lisa spoke by phone every night. The three-hour time difference meant Lisa would be up until after midnight talking with him. One night, after asking her to hang up and go to bed several times, David went into her room, confiscated her phone, took it with him into his bedroom, and closed the door.

Lisa got so angry that she cut herself several times with a razor and called the police from the kitchen phone, telling them that her dad was attacking her with a knife. The next thing David knew, he was awakened by three police cars screaming to a stop in front of his house with lights and sirens blaring.

He ran downstairs in his underwear, and as soon as he opened the door, two policemen grabbed him and threw him onto the hood of one of the police cars, face down and spread-eagle.

They handcuffed him, and as we have all seen on television, shoved him into the back seat while pushing his head down so he didn't hit his head on the door frame. In the meantime, neighbors were coming out of their houses to watch.

At this point, Lisa got scared and ran downstairs screaming that her father hadn't done anything.

By now, another siren was piercing the calm, balmy Georgia night as an ambulance pulled up to take Lisa to the emergency room for her cuts. They treated the cuts, which were superficial, on the spot and allowed Lisa to go with her dad to the police station, where everything was eventually sorted out.

When Lisa and David returned home around dawn, David, utterly defeated, slumped on the stairs, and through tears said, "Lisa, I just can't do this anymore."

The next day, he put her on a plane back to Houston. The five weeks she had spent with her dad had not been a magic pill, as Bill had hoped. She had indeed given him as much grief as she had given us. *Perhaps more.*

Chapter 33

Throw Momma from the Car

I took very little satisfaction from knowing that David had experienced no more success than we had. For a fleeting moment, though, I was relieved that I wasn't the problem—that no matter who took care of her, she still was self-destructive, impulsive, and defiant.

I also felt empathy and to a large extent, sympathy, towards Lisa's father. I think he tried his best to help her and really believed he could. That's why he was so devastated when he discovered he couldn't.

The relief and empathy I felt were short-lived because here we were again, needing to find an educational environment that was appropriate for Lisa, except that this time we were really under the gun time-wise. It was already the end of August, and most schools were beginning their terms.

Brian was getting ready to start college about two hours away and was moving into a dorm. Bill and I were scheduled to begin another semester teaching at the community college in a week and were busy with advising students, registration, and meetings. I essentially missed most of the first two weeks of teaching my classes.

First, I took a day off to help Brian move into his dorm. I was not going to miss the parental gratification and fulfillment of sending a child off to college. Brian had been such a good kid, and although he didn't work as hard as he should have in school, he was highly intelligent and I was proud to be sending him off to further his education. My tears flowed freely as I drove away, as I'm sure they do for all moms whose nests would be more lonely and quiet, no matter how many children might still be at home.

Then I concentrated on Lisa's needs in a series of visits to Atlanta, Connecticut, Rhode Island, and Austin. First, I flew to Atlanta to meet with the psychologist at the hospital where Lisa had stayed and with the educational consultant David had found.

I immediately felt comfortable with the consultant. She was clearly invested in helping us help Lisa, and she was knowledgeable about the options that the mental health professionals felt were best for troubled teens like Lisa. *David had done well in finding her.*

The consultant had researched and familiarized herself with seven different residential treatment programs that she felt were appropriate. She had visited most of them herself at one time or another, so she was able to give David and me detailed information. The cost seemed to be about the same for each, anywhere from $5,000 to $6,000 per month. The good news was that our insurance would probably pay for 50% of that—*probably*—with enough documentation.

Of the seven facilities, only one was in Texas. The rest were scattered about the country in Utah, Montana (*uh-uh—been there, done that*), Idaho (*not much better than Montana*), Tennessee, Connecticut, and Rhode Island.

Lisa's dad and I flew first to Providence, Rhode Island, to check out the facilities there, and then planned to drive to a small town in Connecticut right across the border. We were given tours at both places and decided that neither was appropriate for Lisa. Rhode Island was more of a juvenile boot camp, which was not the proper approach for someone with Lisa's problems, and Connecticut was not a contained facility, had no locks, and was on the honor system with its attendees. *Honor system? Definitely not for Lisa.*

To say that David and I were frustrated would be the understatement of the year. We were desperate and exhausted and began to take it out on each other. The stress of behaving civilly toward each other for our daughter's sake had taken its toll. While in the rental car, driving back to the Providence airport, we argued and blamed and accused each other until he stopped the car on the side of the road in the middle of nowhere and instructed me to get out.

I had no idea where we were because I had been too busy slinging accusations and deflecting blame to watch the road. I knew I had no desire to stand on the side of the road and try to hitch a ride in the 90-degree heat, so I defiantly shot back, "You are not going to throw me out of this car. I refuse to go. Let's just calm down and get to the airport." We rode in fuming silence the rest of the way.

Chapter 34

Right under My Nose

One of the residential treatment centers recommended by the consultant was outside of Austin, only a three-hour drive from Houston. It was my next visit. Neither David nor I wanted to be in the same car again, so this time Bill arranged for a substitute professor to teach his accounting classes, and he accompanied me.

The seventy-acre hospital and residential treatment campus was located in a scenic, wooded hillside and had been in operation for almost sixty years. It specialized in treating adolescents and young adults who presented treatment challenges and who have not had success in other settings. The staff's philosophy was never to give up on a patient. If a particular method was not benefitting a patient, strategies would be evaluated and new approaches developed. They prided themselves on developing innovative, individualized treatments.

The list of difficulties to which they had successfully applied therapeutic interventions included emotional disturbances, severe learning disorders, severe impulsiveness, aggressive behavior, unprovoked mood swings, explosive/suicidal/self-abusive behaviors, substance abuse, seizure disorders, and neurological disorders.

Bill and I were impressed and felt that the program was a perfect fit for Lisa. It had been right under our noses all the time, only 150 miles from our home. At this point, though, after all of the disappointments, I refused to get excited. This could turn out to be just another failed endeavor. On the other hand, there was something different about this place. I had a good feeling about it.

Bill and I completed some paperwork regarding insurance, so that the business office could verify coverage. The business manager reported to us that after a deductible, our insurance company would cover 50% of the $375 per day charge. This left about $180 per day, or $5,400 per month for us to pay ourselves.

Four years earlier in our divorce settlement, David and I had agreed to divide both children's medical expenses equally. As a result, he would be paying half of the expenses at Six Meadows. I had to decide if I could afford the $2,700 per month I would be responsible for. It was almost all of my after-taxes, take-home pay as a community college professor, but I saw no other option.

The next Monday (I had to take yet another day of leave), Lisa and I drove to Austin to admit her into Six Meadows Treatment Center.

The amount of paperwork I had to sign in the business office was staggering. There was an application for voluntary admission, consent to treat forms, treatment planning objectives, permission to transfer levels of care, patient rights, authorization for medical treatment, consent for HIV testing, consent for flu vaccine, administration of birth control pills, release form for ROPES course and swimming, authorization for photographing and videotaping, and several authorizations for release of records. I also had to provide her immunization record and a copy of my divorce decree from David.

My mind was in a daze and on autopilot as I completed all the tasks. I was briefed on visitation and telephone rules, and I met the counselors, nurses, and other personnel who would be with my daughter on a constant basis. We discussed my participation in family therapy sessions, which I said I would be happy to do. Meanwhile, Lisa was meeting the staff and some of the residents in another area.

When I was ready to leave, Lisa was brought back to the business office to say good-bye. She was excited and seemed happy. She described the "store" where she would be able to purchase rewards for good behavior and even progress to the point when she could "work" there and dispense items to other residents. She thought the facilities were beautiful and that her roommate was nice.

She was perhaps most excited about showing me a display case of a variety of stuffed animals. She explained that when she is able to leave Six Meadows, she will be allowed to select a stuffed animal to take home. She already had one picked out, she said.

I think she believed that her stay here would be as short as the ones at the wilderness camp and in New Mexico had been. My gut told me otherwise. Something about the determined and professional demeanor of everybody involved in the treatment center told me they were never going to give up on her because they could handle anybody.

Our good-bye was upbeat and optimistic. We hugged and kissed, and I promised to write and call and visit as much as I was allowed. Still in somewhat of a mental fog, I walked to my car, drove off campus, pulled over to the side of the street, and cried.

I was grieving the loss of Lisa's adolescence. She had just turned fifteen years old, and instead of enjoying parties and sleepovers, having curfews, going to football games, trying out for cheer squad, or going to the junior prom, she would be in a locked facility, trying to learn how to control her impulses and emotions.

I was also grieving for myself—the loss of the hopes and dreams I had had. I would not be doing what other mothers of fifteen-year-old girls were doing. I would not be taking her to parties or sleepovers or to football games. I would not be going shopping with her to pick out new clothes. I would not be arguing with her about the amount of make-up she was wearing or being on the phone too much.

Then there was the doubt and the guilt. Was I doing the right thing? Was I abandoning her? I was racked with guilt that I had somehow failed as a parent. I was being forced to admit that I couldn't keep my daughter safe. Indeed, I couldn't. That was the main reason she was going to Six Meadows—to be safe. As much as I hated leaving her in that hospital prison, at least I knew she would be safe there. *I had no choice. I had no choice. I had no choice. I wasn't abandoning her—I was keeping her safe.*

I pulled myself together, inserted a Beach Boys music tape, and drove to a nearby gasoline station to buy a cup of coffee and fill up the car with gas for the lonely three-hour drive home.

Chapter 35

Hit the Ground Running

This school meant business and wasted no time. Within the first forty-eight hours of admission, Lisa had a mental status evaluation, neuropsychological consultation, medical history and physical examination, residential admission assessment, educational testing, and a nursing assessment.

The admission assessment was straightforward. It was done by a licensed psychologist and was what had previously been called a psychological assessment when administered to Lisa many times in years past. Unlike the others, which had been lengthy, vague, and general, this one was brief and nailed the issues and what needed to be done:

"The reason for placement is patient's suicide attempts, defiance and impulsivity, and the dangerous and self-destructive behavior in which she engages. Immediate and long-term goals are keeping her safe, helping her make responsible decisions, control her impulses, and take responsibility for her behavior."

That certainly described it in a nutshell.

The mental status evaluation was performed by the school psychiatrist, Dr. Robbins, to determine if her mental functioning was adequate to participate in treatment. His report stated that although Lisa was well-groomed and wearing appropriate clothing upon admission, she was uncooperative, evasive, and guarded in attitude. She seemed to have little recognition of her problems, no idea about what to do about them, and seemed unmotivated to participate in treatment. However, since she had no disturbances in thought content, perception, or speech, her mental functioning was deemed adequate for treatment.

The medical history uncovered her past suicide attempts and self-harm incidents, but overall her physical examination was within normal limits, with the exception of her enuresis. Her past medications were listed as Anafranil, Wellbutrin, Zoloft, Ritalin, and Verapamil.

The nursing assessment documented her current medication as Depakote, 250 mg in the morning and 1,000 mg at bedtime. The nurse also identified her frostbite and previous ankle surgery and defined her several attempts at suicide, among them, drinking Triaminic cough syrup, cutting her wrists, and tying a shoestring around her neck. Her height and weight were listed as five feet, five inches and 136 pounds. She also stated that Lisa needs to wear glasses but refuses.

The Woodcock-Johnson Educational Battery, a highly-regarded intelligence test, was administered to Lisa for her educational assessment. She scored in the 40th percentile of students her age in reading and written language, but only in the 6th percentile in math. The recommendation of the counselor was special education assistance under the categories of learning disorder and emotional disturbance.

A neuropsychologist, a specialist in the area of brain-behavior relationships, performed the neuropsych testing. Over the previous years Lisa had undergone numerous, repetitive psychological tests, none of which was particularly helpful in determining a root cause of her disorder to guide effective treatment methods for her. The neuropsych data from this testing, however, was expected to provide specific information that could lead to an accurate diagnosis of her deficits and subsequent rehabilitation.

The fact that she was getting this testing reinforced my satisfaction with putting Lisa in Six Meadows. Finally, we were moving forward and not just repeating the same tests over and over, hoping for different results. *In fact, didn't Einstein define insanity as doing the same thing over and over again but expecting different results?*

Ten days later, I returned to Six Meadows to meet with the treatment team to go over the neuropsychological testing results. The neuropsychologist who conducted the tests was an outside consultant, so I felt comfortable about his objectivity when recommending treatment.

I was impressed to learn that the newest technique of neuroimaging to map the electrical impulses in her brain had been used. Neuroimaging has been shown to distinguish a variety of disorders such as epilepsy, learning disabilities, depression, schizophrenia, dementia, head trauma, and organic brain disease. In addition, it would rule out a brain tumor as a cause for her symptoms.

I was handed one page that had about a dozen brain images on it and an official report, which simply said, "Excessive and aberrant reactivity in both hemispheres as well as absent and abnormal cognitive responses." The words aberrant and abnormal were piercing but vague, so I was anxious to have the professionals explain exactly what they meant.

The psychologist explained that Lisa had a neurodevelopmental disorder. Her brain activity was abnormal in all major cortex sections of the brain, affecting every aspect of her mental functioning except for vision and memory. He explained that deficiencies in the bilateral frontal lobe result in impulse control and attention deficits, and abnormalities in the left frontal lobe manifest in depression.

Her most serious impairment, however, was in the right frontal lobe, which is considered our emotional control center and home to our personality.

This was beginning to sound like the borderline personality disorder that Lisa's psychiatrist back in Houston talked about.

The frontal lobes are responsible for "higher" brain functions, such as planning, decision making, and judgment, which together are called "executive functions." The frontal lobes are also responsible for regulating, checking, and inhibiting emotions and actions.

As a result, people with impairment in this area are impulsive, moody, agitated, easily irritable, explosive, have difficulty concentrating, make poor decisions because of their reasoning inability, and behave inappropriately in social situations. In addition, statistics show that they are quite vulnerable to becoming substance abusers.

This was a seminal moment. The brain imaging showed that she has a biological, physiological abnormality. I can't take her actions personally, nor should I feel personally responsible for her actions. It wasn't something I was doing wrong. She had brain impairment.

Okay, she can't help her actions, and I'm not to blame for poor parenting. I'm off the hook. But, what can we do about it? Is she just doomed to go through life with wild mood swings, poor judgment, and all the other things they mentioned, or is there something we can do?

The treatment team then began to explain their plan for Lisa. Her treatment would be similar to that for a person who has received a traumatic brain injury in an accident. Long-term training—not therapy, per se—would be needed to teach her social skills and anger management to reduce her self-destructive behavior.

This training would need to be done in a highly structured, residential behavior management program. Family therapy would not be needed because her problems were neurological and neurodevelopmental; in other words, her problems were due to a brain impairment and not to family dysfunction.

As a result of the testing, Lisa's primary diagnosis was pervasive developmental disorder, with borderline personality features, and cerebral dysrhythmia. Co-morbid, or simultaneous, diagnoses remained the same as when she was admitted: impulse control disorder, ADHD, enuresis, math disorder, and learning disorder. Her GAF, or functioning level, was determined to be at 35%. Her mood-stabilizing medication was changed from Depakote to Tegretol. Although they are similar medications, Tegretol had been shown to be more effective in decreasing self-destructive behaviors.

After all of the testing was completed, the next step was a master treatment plan to be immediately drawn up by the treatment team: her primary therapist, the medical director, unit director, unit nurse, speech pathologist, dietician, psychologist, director of education, director of recreation, and the substance abuse therapist.

Of course, Lisa didn't wait for any treatment plan. By the time staff were able to formulate the treatment plan, about ten days after her arrival, she had already been placed on the "high precautions" level because of her actions.

Her therapist informed me on the phone that on one occasion Lisa had mutilated herself and could not be calmed down. Her therapist went on to say that Lisa would go a day or two with appropriate behavior, and then something would distress her and she would be unable to calm herself down.

For example, when Lisa realized she could not have her special treat at the end of the day due to her own mistakes, she was inconsolable and ended up in seclusion. She was requiring close monitoring by staff because her impulsivity and lack of ability to manage painful feelings were leading her to escalate rapidly to self-abuse.

Because she was considered a danger to herself, the treatment plan called for three months of 24-hour skilled supervision to monitor her behavior and her medications. *In other words, to keep her safe.*

The long-term goal was to discharge her in three months with an ability to manage her difficult feelings with self-calming techniques and an ability to talk about them with others. In the short-term, a behavior shaping program would attempt to reduce the frequency of self-harming actions. One of the strategies listed was to give her special treats each day that she is able not to harm herself. Lisa's treat of choice was a package of Ramen noodles.

This sounded so weird. A treat for NOT harming oneself. I guess this is what they meant about her need for training instead of therapy, at least initially.

The staff and I set up a plan for telephone conferences to keep me advised and a schedule for on-site visits with Lisa.

Chapter 36

The "Plan" Begins

Lisa's treatment plan focused on three main problems. The first problem was inappropriate affect management, which simply meant that Lisa's expression of emotion was extreme when reacting to a situation. She would become depressed, angry, or hostile and look for ways to hurt herself physically (cutting, banging her head, pulling her hair out) in order to feel pain on the outside as opposed to the inside. She was very aware that she needed to stop this behavior, but she couldn't resist the impulse because it was so strong. The goal was for Lisa to talk out her emotional pain rather than harm herself.

During her first month at Six Meadows, staff observed 59 episodes of inappropriate reactions, including self-abuse, so she was on 24-hour supervision.

The second problem on which focus was placed was Lisa's inability to control her behavior. Whenever she was angry, depressed, or distressed, she responded with lying, impulsivity, poor judgment, and manipulation. Staff noted 231 episodes of behavioral problems during the first month. These resulted in special treatment procedures, or STP's, of three locked seclusions, three mechanical restraints, and three physical holds. These STP's were utilized only when Lisa was at significant risk to injure herself or others. Each time she would receive counseling on how to self-manage difficult situations.

Her dysfunction at home was the third problem. The defiance and the impulsive behavior that would place her in dangerous situations were the main reasons we couldn't manage her at home. Before she could leave Six Meadows, she would have to demonstrate the ability to abide by parental rules.

During the first month I visited her twice, and her dad visited her three times. The visits went well for all of us. Lisa seemed to enjoy them and in fact reported to staff that she had enjoyed seeing us. During these visits, we were given the use of a cheery meeting room with windows along one wall. There were tables and chairs that we used to play board games, draw, or do arts and crafts. In addition to visits, her dad and I each called her several times a week.

During the next three months of October, November, and December of 1997, Lisa showed marked improvement in the number of affect and behavior management incidents, but she still threatened to kill herself on numerous occasions and attacked staff members when they tried to intervene.

Lisa's behavior management showed some progress by November in that she finally admitted that she often lies in order "to not look like an idiot" after she self-abuses. For example, she had justified her self-abuse by saying that she overheard her stepfather calling her a "bitch" when she was talking to me on the phone, which was a complete lie.

She wrote letters weekly that begged me to take her out of the treatment center, and they tore my heart out, but I recognized that she was trying to manipulate me.

In early December, I distracted her with plans for her Christmas pass. I told her that if she improved her behavior enough to earn a pass, the entire family—Lisa, Bill, her brother Brian, and I—would fly to California to visit her stepbrother.

These plans gave her something to focus on for the next few weeks, and she succeeded in earning a one-week Christmas pass.

As planned, during the week between Christmas and New Year, Lisa, Brian, Bill, and I flew to California to visit Bill's son and his wife. The week was filled with activities that Lisa enjoyed, such as the Tournament of Roses Parade, the San Diego Zoo, and New Year's Eve festivities.

I made sure that Lisa took her medications as scheduled, and most of her behavior throughout the visit was appropriate. She was still hyperactive and impulsive, had trouble sleeping, and was resistant to the limits we set; nonetheless, I considered the pass to be a success.

Unfortunately, soon after she returned to Six Meadows, there was significant regression. During January and February of 1998, staff described Lisa as being extremely volatile with frequent tantrums and incidents of self-abuse. She was unable to adhere to limits, seeing them as rejections, and she was unable to tolerate feedback regarding her behavior.

In January she had 339 behavior incidents (compared with 231 the first month), and in February she incurred 467. Things seemed to be going the wrong direction. Her estimated discharge was delayed by three more months, and Tegretol was added to her medications, which already included Zoloft and Anafranil for depression, Depakote for mood stabilization, Ritalin for ADHD, and as needed for severe agitation, Thorazine.

I was only able to visit her on campus twice during these two months. Two other visits had to be canceled by the school because Lisa was "on structure." This meant that her behavior was not satisfactory enough to earn a pass.

On the two weekends she was allowed visitors, Lisa's grandmother (my mother) accompanied me on one occasion, and Bill accompanied me on the other. Both times, I brought along Lisa's dachshund, Heidi. I brought a bucket of fried chicken with the trimmings, and we had a "picnic" while watching some videos that I had brought. I also brought books, snacks, and stuffed animals for her to keep with her in her room.

She seemed tired both times and had little energy although she was very excited to see us—especially Heidi—when we arrived. As our time to leave approached, however, she would withdraw and even suggest that we leave early. It was as if she wanted to get the unpleasantness of saying good-bye over with.

She didn't say much about her life at Six Meadows. I tried to get her to open up about her friends, the staff, her activities, but she shut down when I did. She was still having difficulty communicating her thoughts and feelings to me. This was an area that her therapists continued to address.

As for me, I felt strangely relieved after these visits. I was able to see through the gloom that had been pervading my life. I could see that Lisa was learning about boundaries and responsibility. I could see personal growth and ability to better deal with her feelings, despite the regressions she was experiencing in treatment. But most of all, she was safe. *Most of all, she was safe. The peace of mind that knowledge brought me was indescribable.*

The spring months of March through June were better, and her GAF (level of functioning) was raised to 42% with therapy notes stating "Lisa has not self-abused in over six weeks and is learning to express her feelings with others in an appropriate non-attention-seeking manner. Lisa knows she is prone to throwing tantrums when not utilizing her coping mechanisms and has expressed a desire to eliminate these. She even gave supportive feedback to a peer about how to express her emotions. Lisa has continued positive-attitude worksheets to help identify thinking errors. She is well-behaved in group therapy and confronts peers appropriately when they misbehave."

Lisa's dad and I continued to visit her as often as we were allowed. We also talked with her on the phone several times a week. Only occasionally now did a visit have to be canceled or she was not allowed to take a call because she was "on struc-ture."

During these visits and calls, Lisa was beginning to share her thoughts and feelings with us and seemed to be more accept-ing of herself and her need for treatment. We also had frequent conferences with Lisa's primary therapist, who related that Lisa was continuing to progress.

Then suddenly, in July, she experienced another difficult pe-riod of 547 behavioral transgressions, a record high for her. Her GAF was lowered from 42% to 38% as she regressed to old, negative, attention-seeking behaviors. She also struggled with staff and became physically aggressive. On several occasions she attempted to hit them with her fists, needing to be restrained and secluded.

One step forward and two steps back.

Chapter 37

Sweet Sixteen

Despite her intensive treatment, Lisa's life—and ours—remained a roller coaster. I don't know if there is medical research to support it, but adolescence seemed to exacerbate her destructive impulsivity and her inability to tolerate negative emotions like anger. In addition to the behaviors caused by her illness, she was experiencing the normal teen angst and hormones. Added together, they made her emotions go even wilder and much harder to cope with.

Lisa's conduct seemed to improve after she was told that she would not be allowed to have a two-week home pass at the end of August for her sixteenth birthday unless she showed improvement. She began to work diligently. She talked out her feelings in therapy and showed patience with her peers, even those that seemed to try to provoke her to anger. She dropped the number of behavioral episodes to 154, with one major transgression when she was discovered to be talking "through the wall" to a male resident who was in seclusion, making inappropriate sexual comments.

For this infraction she was placed in AP, or Adult Protection. This treatment designation required her to sleep in the well-

142

lighted hallway outside her room so that staff could see her at all times.

She quickly worked herself off AP into level one and then quickly into level two, where she needed to be to acquire her two-week home pass.

Lisa was eagerly waiting for me as I arrived at Six Meadows on the first day of her pass. I was briefed by staff on rules and treatment goals that she should be following while on her pass. We also discussed that Lisa had brought up an issue in one of the trauma groups with regard to being afraid of going on pass. She stated in group that she was feeling stressed about boys being at her birthday party. The group gave her feedback, and she was instructed to tell her family that no boys needed to be at her party. In addition, I was instructed that if Lisa acts out while on this pass, I should bring her back to treatment immediately, even if the pass has not yet expired.

Lisa spent the first few days of her pass with her father, who reported no unusual struggles. She seemed to be in a honeymoon period of sorts as she transitioned from the treatment center back to her home environment.

After her dad returned to Atlanta, Lisa and I focused on planning her sixteenth-birthday party. I made sure that she took her medication properly and got plenty of sleep. I made one exception to her medication regimen. If her behavior was appropriate and she didn't seem irritable or hyperactive, I did not dispense her Ritalin.

Lisa invited four female friends to her "Sweet Sixteen" party, which was very low-key. The girls seemed to have a good time listening to music, dancing, talking, and gorging on food and soft drinks. One of her closest friends then spent the night.

There were incidents during the pass, of course. I caught her trying to steal money from my purse. She ignored limits I set and at times acted needy and clingy.

When it was time to return to Six Meadows, however, Lisa did not resist or act out. Afraid that she would try to run away to avoid going back to the treatment center, I was constantly vigilant of her actions. She actually seemed eager to return, however. There was something about being in complete charge of herself away from the treatment center that scared her. Six Meadows was a safe, structured environment that, on some level, she now realized she wanted and needed.

When I took her back to Six Meadows, the staff and I held a short briefing to discuss the pass, and I mentioned that it had gone smoothly most of the time, but that there were still rough patches. Because Lisa had returned with 29 Ritalin pills, I was admonished for not requiring Lisa to take all of her Ritalin doses.

A staff member told me, "Maybe if you had given her the Ritalin as prescribed, the pass would have gone more smoothly."

I chose not to argue, but I did not regret my decision. I strongly believed that if Lisa could function near-normally without Ritalin, I wouldn't make her take it. She was not in school while she was on pass, so she didn't have to concentrate on lessons. She was on a "vacation" of sorts, and I wanted to see if she could get by without it. Both she and I did get by without it.

The next month's treatment report stated that Lisa had been "exhibiting problems and been inconsistent in her efforts to work treatment" after returning from her pass. This was attributed to "not taking her medications while on pass."

When I read this, I became angry. It sounded as if she had taken *none* of her medication. It made me look as though I were a terrible mother who neglected her child's medical needs. I had taken great pains to make sure Lisa ingested every one of her handfuls of pills as she was supposed to. The only pill I hadn't given her on occasion was the Ritalin, and that wouldn't have had anything to do with any problems she had after returning to the facility.

Another entry in the monthly report stated that despite being told that Lisa didn't want any boys at her party, I allowed her to have boys attend. This was untrue, and I can only suspect that it was Lisa who told staff that story to justify her attempt at self-abuse two days after returning.

One week after her sixteenth birthday, Lisa had an anniversary. She had been in treatment at Six Meadows for a year.

Her original treatment plan had called for three months of treatment and then a step-down program. But Lisa's repeating pattern of improvement followed by regression, coupled with rocky home visits, caused her safety to remain an issue. She still had to be placed on suicide precautions occasionally, she continued to self-mutilate, and she still had a tendency to become oppositional defiant in response to limits or directives.

These documented episodes allowed continuing coverage by our insurance, but we were told to be ready with a less restrictive "step-down" program for Lisa to attend as soon as she was discharged from Six Meadows. *In other words, as soon as insurance stopped paying, she was outta there.*

In November, after a total of fourteen months in treatment, Lisa was given a pass to travel with me to Alabama to look at New Heights, a private, therapeutic boarding school that was recommended by the staff at Six Meadows. They described the school as being an outdoor program structured to address behavioral problems, unlike the therapeutic schools we had tried earlier, who were not equipped to address such problems.

The purpose of the trip was for Lisa, her father, and me to look at the school and for the school to assess Lisa's appropriateness for their program. Lisa's father met us in Alabama, where we drove to New Heights. The campus was set on wooded acreage with mountains, brooks, and wildlife. We toured the cottages where residents stay and observed some of the activities and classes. David and I were interviewed by the headmaster first, and then Lisa was interviewed.

Lisa seemed comfortable with the environment and expressed delight that she would be near her father, who lived in Georgia. Because of our negative history with such therapeutic boarding schools, David and I had the foresight to maintain a guarded attitude about the facility and try to keep Lisa from becoming too excited about the prospect of attending New Heights.

It was good that we did.

New Heights did not accept Lisa. She was not accepted at their group care facility, nor was she accepted at their locked facility due to her acting-out behaviors. They decided that she would not be able to manage her behavior in a less restrictive setting.

Lisa was disappointed, but she handled the news fairly well. She, her therapist, and David talked about the decision that New Heights had made. Lisa seemed to comprehend that she would have to work harder on self-management. She would need to improve the control of her impulsivity and self-abusive behaviors if she ever expected to leave Six Meadows, where she had already been for fifteen months.

Back at Six Meadows, David and I visited her on alternate weeks. She was now allowed to go off campus, so we went to movies, shopped, picnicked, ate at her favorite restaurants, and visited nearby friends. Occasionally, I would bring along her closest childhood friend, Ashley. Both girls enjoyed those visits immensely.

While out on pass, I would talk with her about how her behaviors had an impact on herself and on others. Lisa and I practiced a thinking-ahead procedure she had learned at Six Meadows, "If I _____ now, then _____ will happen." Cause and effect relationships had always been impossible for Lisa to understand, going all the way back to when she couldn't understand what would happen to her if she ran into a busy street until the graphic impression of a bloody head was used.

As we drove around, we would practice. If I don't stop at this stop sign, what will happen? If I spend all my money in this store and then don't have enough gasoline to get home, what will happen? If I don't get you back to Six Meadows in time, what will happen? If you act out at the movie, what will happen?

At the end of her fifteenth month at Six Meadows, Lisa was referred for another psychological assessment with hopes of placing her in a less restrictive setting. She was forthcoming in her responses to the examiner's questions and offered significant information without prompting. She said she knew nothing about her biological parents, but described me, her adoptive mother, as tall, fun to be with, caring, understanding, and strict when I needed to be. She went on to say that David, her adoptive father, was funny and strong and that she was closer to him than to me. *That one stung a little.*

She mentioned David's and my divorce and stated that she blamed herself for the divorce until recently. She admitted being angry when I remarried and admitted to lying about Bill abusing her. She reported that she now accepts the divorce and gets along with her stepfather.

This was the psychologist's summary:

"Early in her treatment at Six Meadows, Lisa was often self-abusive and required special treatment procedures and safety precautions. She was gradually able to work through her feelings about her parents' divorce and stopped blaming herself. Her frequency of self-abuse has decreased significantly, and she has improved in her ability to think ahead by considering the consequences of her behavior. She last scratched her arm two weeks ago and related the incident to her anxiety about transferring to a new school and being around people she does not know.

Lisa has made significant progress in her treatment at Six Meadows and appears ready to transfer to a less restrictive setting. She will continue to require supervision and intervention when she is unable to cope with stressful situations. Brief placements into an acute psychiatric facility may become necessary to help her to regain control when she is reacting dangerously to stressful situations. Her deficits may require remaining in a structured treatment program until she is able to live independently."

So there it was—official recommendation to transfer Lisa to a step-down, or less restrictive, facility. Her "numbers" had improved: only 119 behavioral episodes for the month of December, and her GAF level of functioning was back up to 40% after being at 38% for the previous seven months.

Lisa came home on a two-week pass for Christmas, during which time I continued to search for an appropriate facility she could attend after her estimated discharge date from Six Meadows the next month, January, 1999. I talked over the telephone with representatives from ten different residential therapeutic schools in five different states.

Some of them would not accept her because of her diagnoses, and some said to call them again "when Lisa completes her next school or accomplishes all that she can." In other words, she wasn't quite ready for them yet. *Actually, they weren't ready for her.*

I was happy, however, that the schools were being honest with me. We had already made so many site visits to places that later turned us down, and of course there were the two disastrous placements in Montana and New Mexico. I wanted to be sure this time that the next facility was suitable for her needs.

One of the residential schools seemed to be a good fit for Lisa. It was a "community home" that was actually associated with Six Meadows and located about a two-hour drive from the Six Meadows campus. Hillside School had been the step-down program for numerous "graduates" of Six Meadows, who went on to lead productive lives.

I spoke at length with the headmaster of Hillside and was satisfied that they were adequately knowledgeable of Lisa's history and her needs. They had full access to her records since they were associated with Six Meadows; therefore, there would be no surprises for them. It was agreed that someone from Hillside would interview Lisa at Six Meadows and that an appointment would be made for Lisa to visit the Hillside Campus as soon as possible.

Lisa's time at home during her two-week Christmas pass was wonderfully uneventful. Her brother was on break from college, so he and Lisa spent the first week of her pass with their dad in Atlanta. They returned home on Christmas Day, when we celebrated our family Christmas. The remainder of the week was filled with dentist and eye appointments and two movies she wanted to see, <u>Antz</u> and <u>Babe</u>.

Her choice of two children's movies verified how immature she still was.

Chapter 38

Show Me Missouri

During Lisa's Christmas pass, her dentist found seven cavities that needed to be filled. This necessitated a three-day home pass the last week in January so she could get that done. I planned to pick her up at Six Meadows in the morning and before going home, we would drive to Hillside for Lisa's on-campus visit.

Someone from Hillside had already interviewed Lisa at Six Meadows, so they were ready to accept her if, after visiting, she and I agreed.

The residence was surrounded by woods and a large swimming pool. The educational program was structured and individually tailored to each student. The ages of students ranged from fourteen to seventeen. The cost of $4,000 per month would be half of what we were paying at Six Meadows because it was a less restrictive program.

Lisa was not as enthusiastic about the setting as she had been on previous site visits. Perhaps she was jaded from not being accepted at the other schools and tried not to get too excited. I didn't know then that she had already hatched a plan that would keep her from going to Hillside.

Most of the next day of Lisa's long-weekend pass, a Friday, was spent at the dentist's office. She spent the rest of the time chatting online and on the phone with friends. She had several chores that were expected of her, such as walking the dog and setting the dinner table, and she performed these without being reminded. She seemed quite happy and energetic, and I attributed her optimism to being at home and generally feeling better about herself and her upcoming transfer to a less restrictive facility. *I should have known better…If it sounds too good to be true, you can bet it isn't.*

The next morning, Lisa went outside, presumably to walk the dog as I was preparing breakfast. She hadn't returned after a half hour, so I checked her room. I saw that the dog was lying on her bed, but her suitcase was gone. Bill and I rushed outside, but Lisa was nowhere to be seen.

In a panic, we canvassed the neighbors, but none of them had seen her. Bill suggested that we calm down so that we could think rationally about where she might have gone. I didn't think I would be able to calm down, but with Bill's supportive reassurance, I was able to take a moment to slow my breathing and allow the blood to flow from my flushed face.

Once I had composed myself, Bill and I agreed we had to stay objective and use all of the detective skills we had learned from years of watching "NYPD Blue" and other police procedurals on television. *What would Detective Andy Sipowicz do?*

On the TV shows, they would check the phone and e-mail records first, so we did the same thing. We checked our telephone bill from the previous month when Lisa had been home on her Christmas pass. We also went into her e-mail account to see with whom she had been in contact recently.

She had run up an $89 long-distance phone bill during the week she was home at Christmas, and most of those calls were to three numbers in the state of Missouri, of all places, where we knew no one.

I got no answer from two of the numbers but was able to connect on the third with a pleasant, gentle-sounding lady. I explained to her that my daughter was missing and that we had found her telephone number in our phone records.

The lady kindly offered to assist us in any way she could and said that she would contact her nineteen-year-old son, Sam, who was at his part-time job, to see if he knew anything about Lisa. She promised to call us back as soon as possible.

In the meantime, we checked into Lisa's e-mail account and found this message from "captainkirk" with the subject line of "bus to Jefferson city, Missouri."

"Why havn't you got to my house yet? Page me immediately 911 911 911 911 911. Are you going to show up like you said or never show up at all. Why? I don't care about my life anymore, don't worry you'll never have to worry about me...I love you...I'll never be on the internet anymore if you don't page me or call me somehow.

With love, Kenneth"

We called the lady in Missouri back with this new information, and she responded that she had talked with her son, Sam, who was a friend of another nineteen-year-old named Kenneth Graves. Her son said that Kenneth had told him that he (Kenneth) was going to drive down to Texas to pick up a girl he had met online who was in trouble. Kenneth, according to his friend Sam, was going to bring her back to Missouri to "get her away from her terrible situation."

This had to be the same Kenneth who had written the note to Lisa online. Lisa must have sneaked out of the house and met up with him somewhere.

But why? And what was this "terrible situation" she had told Kenneth about?

Sam's mother was extremely helpful. She was somehow able to get the license plate number of Kenneth's pickup truck and gave it to us, along with a description of his pick-up truck.

We now had a good idea of what had happened, so we called the missing persons division of the Houston Police Department and told them that a young man from out of state had taken our emotionally-disturbed daughter—although apparently not against her will—and was driving back to his home in Missouri with her.

We gave the police his license plate number, and they issued a BOLO, which is police-speak for "Be On the LookOut" for someone. They contacted the Texas Highway Patrol and the Missouri Highway Patrol.

Now we had to wait. Except that there was one more thing we had to do. We had to notify Six Meadows of her "elopement." Elopement, in psycho-speak, means to escape, or leave without permission or notification. *Or, in this case, a runaway.*

Since it was a weekend, her therapist had to be paged. The therapist called us back within ten minutes, and we related what had happened. She said we had done the right thing in calling the police and asked if Lisa had taken her medications with her.

I had not even thought about Lisa's medications, so I checked the medicine cabinet. All of her medications were still there.

Her therapist said that we needed to find Lisa as quickly as possible, before she began withdrawing "cold turkey" from the powerful psychiatric medications she was taking: Anafranil, Ritalin, Depakote, Zoloft, and Thorazine. She warned that withdrawal symptoms could include any of the following: agitation, hostility, seizures, confusion, nausea, extreme mood swings, or suicidal thoughts. In addition, there were the potential consequences of being off birth control. I tried not to think of those.

This information certainly added to the urgency of finding her. Feeling the need to do something, I called the lady in Missouri who had been so helpful and asked her if she had any news. She did her best to allay my fears by assuring me that she knew Kenneth well because he had been a friend of her son's for a long time. She had known him to be kind and considerate, although he was somewhat irresponsible and a little slow mentally. She was certain, she said, that he would not harm Lisa. She assured me that he probably really believed that Lisa was in trouble and wanted to rescue her.

Her reassurances made me feel better about Lisa's safety with this young man, but I was still concerned about her medications, especially if she made it all the way to Missouri with him and had to be without them for days on end.

I spent an anxious night and slept little. I didn't know if I wanted the phone to ring or not. *Sometimes, especially where Lisa is concerned, no news is good news.* A phone call in the middle of the night is rarely good. This time, however, a phone call might mean the police had found my daughter safe and sound.

It had been over 24 hours since we had discovered her missing, and she and Kenneth could have made it out of the state by now. *Where was she and why did she leave?* The first question would eventually be answered, but someone with Lisa's mental problems might not be able to explain the second—why she left. It was probably one of those impulsive, no-thinking-ahead, irrational things she couldn't seem to control.

It was a Sunday, and I fixed lunch for Bill and myself, although I wasn't really hungry. Then the phone rang. It was a Texas state trooper saying Lisa had been found, safe.

She and Kenneth had never made it out of Texas because Kenneth's truck had broken down about four hours north of Houston in Nacogdoches, population about 30,000. They had to spend the night in a Nacogdoches motel while the truck was being fixed, and police spotted his license plate in the parking lot of the motel.

The officer told us that Lisa was being taken to a local hospital because she had told them she hadn't taken her medication for two days and was feeling "funny." She would be at the hospital, waiting for us to pick her up. Kenneth was being taken to the police station for questioning.

Bill and I quickly packed a small bag in case we had to spend the night and then drove to Nacogdoches, arriving just before dark. Lisa was in the emergency room, entertaining the medical personnel with God-only-knows-what-kind-of stories. I know this because several of them told me what a darling daughter I had. *I wanted to strangle her.*

As had happened numerous times in the past, she looked calm, and I looked like the crazy one as I peppered her with non-stop questions, "What were you thinking? Why did you run away? Do you know what could have happened to you? How could you run away with a perfect stranger? You've known not to do that since you were three years old!"

Of course, her response, as it always was after any irrational, impulsive behavior, was a whiny, "I don't know." *It took me years to understand that she really didn't know.*

She did go on to say that she knew she had made a mistake as soon as Kenneth arrived at the house. She hadn't expected him to actually drive all the way from Missouri to get her. She had maintained a charade with him that she thought was harmless because he was so far away. When he showed up, she felt trapped into having to go with him.

As it turned out, Lisa had been communicating with Kenneth via e-mail and letters since her Christmas pass. They had discovered each other in an online chat room, and Lisa had filled him with invented stories about herself. She had told him that she had a child named Tyler that the State of Texas had taken away because she was in a treatment center. She told him that she was being abused and needed someone to "get her out of there" so she could try to get her child back.

Kenneth believed everything and apparently decided he was going to be her knight in shining armor and rescue her. Sometime later, we found two letters that he had written to Lisa at Six Meadows the month before:

"Lisa, I am waiting for you, my love. I went to the bus station here in Jefferson City three days in a row, but there was no you or Tyler. Sam told me you had called and were on your way. If you cannot come here, I will come and get you. I swear I will get you. I love you eternally. Nothing will change that. I am not mad at you because you didn't show up. When you come up here your life will surely change. You will get over your drug problem up here with me and you will have a place to stay the rest of your life with me no matter what. If you kill yourself, who will Tyler have for a mom? I will always love you forever and will be down there whether I can afford it or not because I love you. Write me back and tell me which weekend I should come down.

I love you forever, Kenneth."

He wrote another letter the next day and mailed it to Six Meadows.

"Hey, Sweetheart. What's up? I am planning my trip to Houston to pick you up. Did the State of Texas say you could get Tyler back when you get a stable life? I hope you are not on probation because I don't want some Texas cop arresting you or me. I don't want some cop interrupting us in the middle of the night either. I will always love you no matter what goes on in your life. I love you with all my heart and more. I miss you a lot. I miss you at nighttime because you are not here in bed with me. If you can't get Tyler back, I will get you pregnant and we will start a new life together. We are still engaged, aren't we, Sweetie? I need to know where you are going to be when I pick you up.

I love you forever, Kenneth."

We never learned what transpired between Kenneth and the police because we never heard from or of him again. *Poor kid. He was naively taken in by Lisa and was just trying to help her. He'd have been in real trouble, though, if he had transported her across the state line.*

156

Chapter 39

Still No Light at the End of the Tunnel

The next day we returned Lisa to Six Meadows, where she was placed on "major elopement risk" for four days and then moved to "elopement watch" for the following week. Of course, in light of her elopement, Hillside changed its mind about accepting her. In addition, David and I were asked to cease visiting her until she was able to maintain level two behavior. Staff felt that she needed the motivation of visits to work effectively in treatment. We were, however, allowed to call her on the phone.

Lisa continued to respond to tension and uncomfortable feelings with anger and hostility. She would climb to the top of her closet, lash out verbally or physically at a peer or staff, or make a self-injurious gesture. When she was held accountable for her behavior, she would tantrum or try to manipulate new staff. Staff was instructed to maintain high behavioral expectations for her despite the fact that she wanted them to believe that she was less capable than she actually was.

Another three months went by. Lisa continued to exhibit either a resistance or fear of assuming age-appropriate behaviors. She would say things like, "I'm afraid of growing up." Indeed, itmay have been this fear of responsibility that led her to sabotage her step-down placement to the less restrictive setting of Hillside by running away with Kenneth.

When she attained level-two status, David and I were allowed to resume our on-campus visits. In clinical teleconferences with staff, we were encouraged to engage her in an age-appropriate manner even when she tried to get us to treat her as a young child.

By April, Lisa began to show signs of being able to manage her feelings and behaviors with periods of maturity and self-calming techniques. The number of behavioral episodes dropped significantly. As a result, she was transferred to a different unit for peers with more developmentally appropriate behavior than those at her previous unit. This was a real step in the right direction!

Lisa worked at finding her role in the new unit and made efforts to connect with the others and share feelings appropriately. However, staff later referred to this initial period as her "honeymoon" with the unit. Soon, her peers began giving her feedback about her immaturity, and her behaviors and self-abusive acting out began to escalate. She was being held to a higher standard of social accountability and as a result, she sought attention in negative ways.

She was placed on high risk of self-abuse and at one point was actually required to wear mittens for several days. She had 501 behavioral episodes during the month of May, including lying, intimidation, threats, defiance, verbal abuse, and self-abuse. She showed little or no motivation to work on her treatment.

During this period, she was on phone restriction, which meant that David and I could each call her only once during the week. She was not allowed to call out. She had now been at Six Meadows for over a year and a half, and I still couldn't see any light at the end of the tunnel. Our insurance was now covering only 20 per cent of the costs, so David's share and my share were each about $3,200 per month. *My entire after-taxes teaching salary.*

But I didn't regret a cent of it. After seeing all the difficulties a professional staff in a locked facility had in treating Lisa, I knew in my heart that she would have ended up dead if she had stayed at home. There was no way I could have controlled her. The past year and a half at Six Meadows kept her alive and gave her practical coping tools to use in the future.

The summer months were a period of mixed results. On the one hand, staff reported that Lisa had made significant improvement in her ability to manage her difficult feelings by self-soothing rather than by manifesting them in behavioral disturbances. They credited that partially to using home visits as a motivational factor plus the fact that she was now writing in a journal to express her thoughts effectively.

However, she was still having difficulty motivating herself and needed external motivation, like the prospect of a home visit. Her behavioral incidents dropped to 351 during the month of June, but rose to 355 in July, and 509 in August, which was the second highest total in her two years at Six Meadows.

On the positive side, however, during these three months, she only required two special treatment procedures (physical holds, seclusions) per month for being at risk of injuring herself or others. She was no longer on mail or phone restrictions, and I was greatly encouraged by her behavior during on-campus and off-campus visits. Her behavior was more consistent, less demanding, and more age-appropriate. She was participating in discussions about her next placement after Six Meadows.

For her home visits, I received guidance from her therapists as to what to expect from her. These home visits, or "therapeutic leaves," as the therapists referred to them, were to be an opportunity for her to act like a young adult and practice at home the skills she had learned in therapy.

For example, I was to enforce a strict 10 p.m. curfew, allow no friends over, keep her in sight at all times, insist on her using an alarm clock to get up in the mornings, let her cook her own breakfast, allow supervised phone calls of no more than ten minutes, require her to care for our dog, as well as make her bed, clean her room, and do her own laundry. If we went shopping, she was to accept all of my decisions. If she became upset, I was told to have her write in her journal, talk it out with me, or take a timeout.

It was a battle to get her to meet all of those expectations, especially cleaning her room. However, she performed well most of the time and rarely used that annoying, whiny, baby voice that she had often reverted to in the past whenever she was upset. She had no cutting incidents, and on only one occasion did I have to revert to a timeout. I had dreaded having to use a timeout because timeouts had never worked in the past. She had no real concept of time, so one minute seemed like twenty to her. Consequently, I often used a one-minute timeout, which seemed to be all it took to break the cycle of her emotional outburst.

Her monthly treatment plan update praised her therapeutic gains, despite the high number of behavioral incidents. Therapists reported that Lisa had successfully overcome her resistance to change by adjusting well to a new roommate as well as several new admissions on the unit. This was a difficult task for her, but she continued to utilize journaling to identify and express her feelings and even attempted to be a role model by offering to help others in areas that she felt she was competent in. She also displayed age-appropriate behaviors 95% of the time and decreased her attention-seeking behavior.

Her therapists also reported another obstacle that may have interfered with treatment progress. Lisa was preparing for possible discharge and was anticipating interviews at other facilities. Because she was anxious about having to accept more responsibility in a new placement, she occasionally regressed to hair-twisting and biting her nails. These, however, were much less self-abusive than past behaviors had been. In fact, during August she had no episodes of attempting to harm herself in any manner.

Lisa's progress in her academic classes had improved as well. Her teacher reported that Lisa was completing all of her assignments in class, maintaining a passing average in each course, and requiring very little prompting to remain on task. She was following directions and maintaining "fair" behavior and interactions in class.

Lisa's seventeenth birthday came in the middle of the week, so we didn't get to celebrate with her until the following weekend. Lisa had earned an off-campus pass, so Bill and I, plus my mom and one of Lisa's friends drove to Austin to eat at a nice restaurant.

I was delighted with her age-appropriate behavior and her discussion of how she has increased her independence by learning skills such as cooking and budgeting. She went on to talk about long-term goals of wanting to work with animals in some capacity. She seemed eager to continue her progress in a less restrictive setting.

I was cautiously hopeful, yet in the back of my mind I fully expected her to do something to sabotage her placement in a step-down program.

Chapter 40

Stepping Down

During this summer-month period, Bill and I had been exploring discharge placements that fit Lisa's needs in the Houston area. She had been accepted by New Pathways Treatment Center, a step-down program that was located only about an hour from our home, but like Six Meadows, it was expensive. Six Meadows had charged $11,000 per month, and our insurance had paid about 50 per cent of that because Six Meadows was considered an inpatient hospital.

New Pathways' charges would be $6,000 per month, but our insurance did not pay for any of it because New Pathways was considered to be a residential facility and not a hospital. So, the cost to Lisa's father and me would actually be about the same.

None of the other facilities we contacted, however, suitably met her needs. Some were similar to Six Meadows and therefore not step-down programs. Others were day treatment facilities, which we felt Lisa was not yet ready for.

Bill and I expressed our financial concerns to the director of New Pathways, and he asked if we had investigated the possibility of financial reimbursement from the school district. Texas law requires all school districts to provide educational services for all children. This means that accommodations must be made to enable students with disabilities to participate meaningfully in learning.

We replied that we had tried for years to get the school district to address Lisa's individual concerns, but their response had been to "throw her into the detention center" with the juvenile delinquents and drug offenders. We went on to explain that even Lisa's psychiatrist had determined that Lisa should not return to the curriculum that had been formulated for her, i.e., the detention center, because it was harmful to her emotional development.

The New Pathways director recommended an attorney who specialized in lawsuits against educational institutions. He had had considerable success in confronting school districts and obtaining reimbursements for parents in the past. Armed with this knowledge and with hopes of perhaps obtaining some financial recompense, Bill, David, and I together made the decision to put Lisa in New Pathways when she was discharged from Six Meadows.

The discharge from Six Meadows Treatment Center came one month after her seventeenth birthday, on September 27, 1999, almost exactly two years from her admission date. The anticipated three-month stay had stretched into two years because even the mental health professionals could not anticipate the challenges she would present.

Lisa's discharge summary that would accompany her to New Pathways summarized her justification for admission as suicidal, violent, impulsive, aggressive, and self-destructive, constituting a danger to herself and others. Her progress was described as slow and vacillating; however, the report went on, "She has increased her ability to use coping skills, problem-solving skills, and has recently begun to see herself as a role model for others." Her condition at discharge was labeled as "marked improvement," i.e., the completion of 75 to 89 per cent of treatment objectives.

Lisa's discharge diagnoses remained mostly the same as they had been two years earlier: pervasive developmental disorder with borderline personality disorder features *(What this meant was that she really had borderline personality disorder, but since she wasn't eighteen years old yet, they had to call it pervasive developmental disorder. Also, very few insurance plans pay for treatment for BPD because it is considered an Axis II disorder. Pervasive developmental disorder is on Axis I, so it is considered an "acute" problem and covered by most plans)*, impulse control disorder, ADHD, nocturnal enuresis, math disorder, nonverbal learning disorder, and cerebral dysrhythmia. The only change was her GAF, or functioning level. It was 36 per cent on admission and was now 45 per cent at discharge.

Only nine percentage points of increased functioning. After two years of treatment totaling $180,000, I expected more. At least she was "well" enough to enter a less restrictive facility. Either that, or there was just nothing more that Six Meadows could do.

Lisa's discharge and aftercare plan recommended that she continue on her medications, which were Anafranil for enuresis, Zoloft for depression, Depakote for mood stabilization, Ritalin for attention deficit and impulsivity, and TriNorinyl for birth control. She was now seventeen years old, her height was still five feet, five inches, and her discharge weight was 152, a gain of sixteen pounds since admission two years ago.

I hired a substitute professor for two days and drove to Austin to pick her up on the day she was discharged. True to their promise two years earlier, staff allowed Lisa to choose a stuffed animal from their collection to remind her of her progress there and of the friends she had made. After good-byes and tears and a little celebration with beverages and cookies, we got into the car and drove home.

I felt relieved, as if a raging river had just been crossed successfully, but I knew there was still a long journey ahead. My daughter and I both had to take things one day at a time, knowing there would yet be many periods of regression to accompany

any progress. But we had a plan and were confident that New Pathways would provide the necessary guidance for Lisa, just as Six Meadows had done.

After a good night's sleep for both of us, the next day Lisa and I drove to New Pathways to enroll her. The best part of New Pathways was its proximity to our home. It was less than an hour's drive away, which I hoped would allow me to participate in staffings, family counseling, and frequent visits.

Like most of the residential facilities we had visited, New Pathways was located in a natural, rural environment. I was beginning to realize why. If patients ran away, they would have a long way to walk to get to civilization. The longer it took, the higher the likelihood that they would be apprehended.

The physical plant consisted of single level residential homes, each with a capacity of eight clients in double occupancy bedrooms. In each therapeutic home there were three bathrooms, a kitchen, dining area, living room, and outdoor recreation area. There were two staff members on 24-hour watch in each home.

I was given Lisa's Individual Service Plan for the residential services she would receive: medical/nursing services daily, continuous behavioral programming, and educational services five days a week by teachers who were all special education-certified. Staff supervision was listed as "high/close proximity" because of her threats of physical aggression, history of suicide, history of runaway and self-injurious behavior. Lisa would also be receiving social skills training daily, individual and group counseling weekly, and family counseling as scheduled by us, her parents. I was satisfied that it was an appropriate placement for my daughter.

I didn't have the usual rock-in-my-stomach feeling that I usually had when I had to leave Lisa in a treatment center and drive away. I guess it was because she was so close to home this time. Also, she was older now and no longer my "baby."

Chapter 41

Taking on the Establishment

The very day that Lisa enrolled in New Pathways and was placed in the eleventh grade, Bill and I began the process of trying to get the public school district (to which we pay property taxes) to share in the cost of Lisa's education. We began with a letter to the director of special education of the school district:

"Dear Sir or Madam:

When Lisa began attending classes in intermediate school of the Deer Lakes School District, she was placed in regular classes despite a documented history of special educational needs. She immediately began having difficulties academically and behaviorally and was assigned additional tutors. This was unsuccessful, so Lisa was assigned to an adaptive behavior classroom. Her behavior and learning deteriorated, and she was placed in an alternative learning classroom with juvenile offenders. This was highly inappropriate for Lisa's special needs, so it was necessary for us to take her out of the public school system and place her in a residential program. For the past two-and-a-half years, Lisa has been educated at our personal expense with no assistance from the school district. However, we strongly believe that the district can and should provide financial assistance for Lisa's education,

166

as the district has been unable to provide her with the services she needs.

Texas State law requires public schools to meet the educational needs of ALL students. Therefore, we ask that you provide us with the necessary forms to begin the petition process and that you advise us as to what documentation you may require."

Three weeks later, we received a response from the director of special education stating that the school district stood ready to perform a comprehensive re-assessment of Lisa's educational needs to determine an appropriate program for her.

The director of special education was new to the district. She was not the same person that had run the department two years ago when we asked for help. The new director was young, energetic, and eager to prove herself. We got the impression that whatever her predecessor had done—or not done—in the past, she was going to fix it for the future.

We asked the attorney—the one that New Pathways had recommended—to begin the process of suing the school district for reimbursement of all of the money we had spent on Lisa's placement in Six Meadows and her current placement at New Pathways. It was our contention that the district had failed to provide a safe environment that addressed our daughter's educational needs in accordance with Texas law.

While the legal wrangling was going on behind the scenes, we cooperated with the school and their never-ending series of ARD meetings. These ARD meetings were ostensibly to determine her educational needs and come up with an appropriate plan.

At the first ARD in early November, 1999, Bill and I came armed with about sixty pages of documents, including evaluations and summaries from each school and hospital that Lisa had spent time in during the past thirty months. The meeting, which was attended by an administrator, two special education teachers,

an instructional specialist, and a psychologist, was long and con-
tentious. We all agreed that Lisa was emotionally disturbed, but
that was about all we agreed on.

We explained the danger that Lisa presents to herself and
others with physical aggression and self-mutilation and insisted
that Lisa could not be educated without the right setting. We
then presented documentation we had just received from New
Pathways about an episode of physical aggression that had required a therapeutic hold the day before. Her teacher noted that
Lisa was highly unpredictable. "She can be absolutely fine one
minute, and then without warning, erupt into rage or aggression," he added. We read the report to the committee and waited
for their response.

One of the school administrators piped up, commenting
that a regular high school setting was probably not appropriate
for her. *Gee, ya think?* The special education teacher then spoke
and explained the school's Significant Intervention Program in
the Special Education Center. She said it was structured with
one-on-one instruction and very similar to what New Pathways
was providing. *How could she know that? She had never even been to
New Pathways. It was all smoke and mirrors.*

Bill and I looked at each other and sighed. We had already
"been there and done that." They didn't respect the fact that we
had already tried every program the public school provided before removing her three years ago. We politely suggested that
school personnel visit New Pathways to observe Lisa, the facilities, and the services they provide.

The meeting ended with official responses for the record
from the school district and from us. The district concluded the
following:

"We feel the district can match educational services and
have a plan that is free and appropriate to meet Lisa's needs. We
have trained teachers to meet her needs in a safe setting. Parents
have requested the district visit the facilities at New Pathways to

gather more information. As a show of good faith, the district will send one of the behavior facilitators, but again, we feel we can meet her needs. We will re-convene in two weeks."

Bill and I wrote the following response into the record:

"While we (Linda and Bill) agree that our daughter requires extensive special education services, we do not agree that the plans submitted by the school district are appropriate because they are inadequate for her needs. She needs the appropriate setting for her education, and based on the danger she poses to herself and others, as well as her runaway risk, we feel that the Special Education Center is not adequate."

I felt frustrated but not desperate because I had good people on my side. My husband, the director of New Pathways, and an attorney were all willing to fight with me for Lisa's well-being.

By this time, Lisa had been at New Pathways for about six weeks. I had attended two staffings, and Lisa had had two successful home visits. It was so wonderful to have her in a school nearby!

She had a boyfriend at New Pathways named Tim. His parents lived about half an hour from our home, so when their passes coincided, Tim's mother or I agreed to supervise them on dates to the mall or the movies.

Lisa was exhibiting success in her academic classes. She was enrolled in English III, math, biology, world history, health, and keyboarding. All of the classes had extensive modifications for her learning disabilities, which allowed her to earn all A's and B's after the first six-week reporting period. She was proud of her report card, and we gushed over her fine record.

Nonetheless, she was still exhibiting some of the same behaviors she had at Six Meadows, including an episode of self-abuse and a suicide attempt whereby she tied a shoe string tightly around her neck in an attempt to strangle herself one night in bed. When the house mother came in to check on her, as she did every thirty minutes, the house mother found Lisa with the covers pulled over her head. When she pulled the covers back, she saw Lisa's face turning blue. The string was so tight that a knife had to be used to remove it.

It was clear that Lisa still needed trained, round-the-clock supervision.

The next ARD, which convened two weeks after the first one, was equally frustrating. This time, the new director of special education was in attendance. Unsmiling but polite, she was beautifully statuesque, in her mid-thirties, and wearing a stylish business suit. She remained quiet and let the other school representatives speak first.

I clenched my jaw as school administration maintained that even after their visit to New Pathways, they were certain they could provide the equivalent educational experience. Bill and I, on the other hand, continued to press the issue of safety in the public school setting and our long history of the public school's failure in that regard.

The instructional specialist added that a home trainer would come to our home to train us in parenting skills and help us "structure and monitor" our home. The psychologist then suggested that we apply through the school district for respite care—a caregiver who would come in and monitor Lisa if we wanted to go out of the house. It was estimated that we might qualify for as much as $3,000 a year to have someone "babysit" Lisa.

The director of special education, who until now had remained stoically silent, finally spoke up. She looked directly at Bill and me and in a firm, controlled voice said, "This is the plan that will stay in place. If you do not agree, you have the option of contacting the Texas Education Agency to have a mediator determine if the services offered are legally appropriate." *In other words, take it or leave it.*

Just as we had two weeks before, we found the school's recommendations naively inadequate, if not downright insulting. *We, the parents, were the ones who needed training? Flashback to the early years when I thought Lisa's problems were all my fault.*

We were given time to compose our official, written response where we stated that a transition to the school from New Pathways would be possible sometime in the future, but that Lisa was not yet ready to leave the safe learning environment of New Pathways. We asked for district financial assistance in the interim.

With nothing resolved and with the tension in the room rising, the ARD was adjourned with the next meeting set for six weeks hence, after the Christmas holidays, in January, 2000. *Does anything move more slowly than this ARD process?*

As it turned out, however, there was no ARD in January because the legal process had begun.

Just before the Christmas holidays, we officially retained legal representation in our lawsuit against the school district. The attorney, Art O'Dell, requested a retainer up front of $8,000, which would be returned to us if we won. He explained that only about 25 - 30 per cent of cases were won outright by parents but that he truly believed we had a strong case and would pursue it to the fullest.

I was hesitant at first about spending all that money on a lawsuit that could prove worthless. Plus, I had always heard horror stories about litigation dragging on for years and ruining people's lives in the process.

Bill felt different, though. He reasoned that the total cost of Lisa's treatment in the past three years had already totaled over $190,000, so why not take a chance on recovering some of that by spending $8,000 more?

The evening we wrote Mr. O'Dell his retainer check, Bill and I phoned Lisa's dad to see if he would like to participate in the lawsuit. He had already spent around $40,000 on Lisa's treatment, and if he was willing to pay half of the retainer, we would share any settlement with him.

Lisa's dad, David, said he was not interested in participating in the legal proceedings, but he wished us luck.

Chapter 42

More Cruise Capers

Bill and I had planned for several months to take the family on a cruise the first week in January, 2000, to celebrate the millennium. By family, I mean Bill and me, Brian and his then-girlfriend Stacy, and Lisa—if she was progressing with acceptable behavior. I discussed with New Pathways staff the possibility of taking Lisa on the cruise, and they felt that it would be a positive experience for her.

I picked up a very excited daughter on New Year's Eve morning from New Pathways. The other students were envious but wished Lisa well and were happy for her. Her boyfriend, Tim, visited her at our home in the afternoon, and Lisa behaved quite well, actually at age-level. Later, she was compliant and helpful in packing and preparing for the trip on New Year's Day.

The five of us climbed into our car and began the six-hour drive to New Orleans, where we boarded the ship for our "millennium cruise" on January 2, 2000. I was worried that Lisa would have difficulties on the long drive, cramped in the back seat with her brother and his girlfriend, but we played travel games and sang the entire way, making the trip pass quickly and enjoyably for all of us.

I was crossing my fingers. So far, so good.

The first day of the cruise was also pleasant, as Lisa continued with good behavior, courtesy, and no attention-seeking actions. She never argued or raised her voice, and we were beginning to think that perhaps she didn't even need to go back to New Pathways!

Tuesday, the second day of the cruise, brought some seemingly innocuous transgressions that I tried to overlook but that nonetheless sounded warning bells for me. For example, each passenger on the cruise was issued an ID/key card that was used not only for identification on the ship and in the ports, but used for charging purchases on board.

We thought about keeping Lisa's card, but we decided to trust her and told her that she was not to use the card to charge anything unless she asked us first.

Lisa came to us at the end of the day and said that she had forgotten the rule and had bought some shampoo at the beauty salon with her card. We forgave this as a legitimate lapse of memory and repeated the instructions. We told her we would give her one more chance.

About this time, Lisa began "borrowing without asking" various articles of clothing from Stacy, who was sharing a room with her. When Stacy told her that it was okay for her to borrow things from her as long as she asked permission first, Lisa sulked. Soon after, Stacy's ID/key card disappeared.

The next morning, the ID/key card mysteriously reappeared on the television set in full view where it would have easily been seen if it had been there all along. Obviously, Lisa had taken it to "get back" at Stacy and then decided for some reason to return it anonymously. However, she vigorously denied taking it. She became loudly defiant when I told her I didn't believe her and would be confiscating her key card for one day.

Later that evening, Lisa took her brother's CD case with about fifty of his CDs out of his room to the main lounge without permission. She forgot them there, and we were very lucky that they were still there several hours later when Brian asked about them. She seemed very upset and embarrassed by this event and refused to associate with any of us for the rest of the evening.

I took all CDs and players away from everyone and locked them in my room. Brian was extremely upset and angry with Lisa, and Lisa blamed me for Brian's anger toward her.

I shouldn't have kept the CDs from Brian, I have since decided. Brian should not have been required to suffer for Lisa's behaviors. There must have been some other consequence for her actions, but I couldn't think of one at the time. I was frustrated and afraid of what the next three days enclosed on a ship would bring.

On Thursday, several people reported to Stacy and Brian that Lisa had been telling "stories" about them all over the ship. I never found out exactly what she said in those "stories," but Brian and Stacy informed me that, among other things, Lisa was telling people that Brian had thrown his CD player overboard. Stacy and Brian confronted Lisa, saying that they were aware that she was telling lies about them and that they did not appreciate it.

Lisa reacted with anger and began yelling and calling Stacy names, saying she didn't want to be her "sister" anymore. When Stacy and Brian walked out of Lisa and Stacy's room, Lisa stayed inside and put the chain guard on the door, refusing to open it for them or anyone else.

By now it was midnight, and we were all in the hallway yelling at Lisa to open the door. Of course, this didn't work, so I sent everyone else away and convinced Lisa to open the door so we could talk. She told me that Stacy had no right to talk to her that way, Stacy was stealing her brother, etc., etc. I had a long talk with her and explained her thinking errors, and she finally calmed down. We all collapsed into bed.

On the last full day of the cruise, Lisa spent most of the day away from all of us with her new friends—all of them younger than she. She appeared occasionally to check in but made it clear she didn't want to be around any of us.

Around 6 p.m. she came to the lounge where my husband and I were dancing and insisted on seeing me immediately. She began to cry and pulled out a wad of receipts from her pocket. She said she had been charging things to her card, which I had returned to her that morning.

Most of the receipts were for soft drinks and food items, but a few were more expensive such as boxes of chocolates and necklaces that she said she gave to her friends. The sum of the receipts was about $80.

Her immediate consequences were that she had to relinquish her card again and then get all the gifts back from her friends. In addition, we decided to take her back to New Pathways on Saturday immediately upon our return home instead of Sunday evening as previously planned. She would also have to repay the money that she spent.

On docking day, Lisa arose when asked and followed all of our instructions immediately and somewhat meekly. The ride home from New Orleans was uneventful, with everyone being forcibly calm and courteous to each other. Lisa listened to music via headphones most of the way. We returned her to New Pathways within an hour of returning home.

Chapter 43

David and Goliath

W hile we were away on the cruise, our attorney had begun the legal ball rolling by filing a request for a due process hearing with the Texas Education Agency. The four-page request outlined in legalese that Lisa was an eligible student with a disability under the Individuals with Disabilities Act and in respect of the Texas Education Code and that we, the petitioners, assert that Deer Lakes School District has violated Lisa's right to a free public education by not providing an appropriate program.

The petition further outlined our requests for reimbursement of the costs and associated expenses for her placements at Six Meadows and New Pathways as well as development of an appropriate transition plan from New Pathways to public school.

Mr. O'Dell had already begun the arduous quest for all of Lisa's medical and educational records. By the end of the month, he would have over 3,000 pages of information. Records from Six Meadows and New Pathways alone filled two large legal-sized paper boxes. The huge volume resulted from the thorough documentation in the treatment centers. Notes about Lisa's behaviors and emotions were written every thirty minutes by staff, plus there were doctor's notes, nurse's notes, therapist's notes, staffing notes, daily reports, monthly reports, quarterly reports, medication notes (every time she was given a medication, it was documented), and on and on.

In the meantime, a mediator had been assigned to our case, and a date of February 7 was set to attempt to resolve the dispute through mediation. It was going to be David vs. Goliath, as our attorney was a solo practitioner who worked out of his home, and the school district's legal representation was a large, prestigious, international law firm with offices in a gleaming downtown Houston high-rise.

The mediation conference was private and confidential, and no notes were allowed to be taken. "Goliath" was there with four attorneys and three school officials. "David" consisted of Bill, me, and Mr. O'Dell.

I was nervous, as the opposition, dressed in their finest silk suits and looking forbidding, smiled smugly across the table. They clearly rejected the notion that the school district had any responsibility whatsoever in reimbursing us for Lisa's private treatment the past two years because the district had not been informed of Lisa's enrollment at Six Meadows. If it had, they maintained, then of course the district could and would have devised an educational plan for her, thus making her stays at Six Meadows and New Pathways unnecessary.

So this was going to be their defense—they didn't KNOW about Lisa's needs before she entered Six Meadows.

I argued that I had indeed contacted the school district soon after Lisa was enrolled in Six Meadows to see what the school district could do for her after the estimated three-month stay at Six Meadows was over. They responded that there was no record of my contacting anyone at the school two-and-a-half years earlier during the fall of 1997.

I was demoralized and angry. I was certain I had contacted the school, but I couldn't prove it. I didn't sleep at all that night, lamenting that our entire case depended on my memory of a phone call that I couldn't prove.

Bill and I met privately with Mr. O'Dell after the mediation procedure to go over our options. Mr. O'Dell seemed happy to know their strategy and said we would go forward in the legal process to the next step, which was a pre-trial hearing.

Mr. O'Dell suggested that in the meantime I should write down as much as I could remember about Lisa's difficulties in the public school, including the times she ran away despite their constant supervision. He also wanted me to go through any and all correspondence, records, and other communication with the school.

I spent the entire weekend on that project. I collected all of the notes and letters from her teachers as well as every note I had made during telephone conferences. Nothing I found, however, supported my contention that I had asked the school for help in the fall of 1997.

Then, suddenly, my eyes spotted something. Tucked away in the kitchen's catch-all junk drawer was one of those telephone memo notes, the ones that say, "While you were out, so-and-so called." It was a message taken by the secretary of my department at Houston Community College on October 15, 1997. It was from the then-director of special education and read, "Margaret Pasternak of the Deer Lakes School District returned your call about Lisa."

There it was! A piece of paper smaller than a blank check proved that I had indeed contacted the school in the fall of 1997. I immediately called Mr. O'Dell and told him about the evidence I had found. I could hear the smile in his voice as he said, "This is the 'smoking gun' that will turn your case around."

Initiating the legal proceedings had indeed lit a fire under school administrators, who shifted into full gear to evaluate Lisa and prepare an educational plan within the public school setting. Suddenly, attention to Lisa was moving lightning-fast, unlike previous years and even unlike the previous semester, when months were wasted waiting on the next ARD committee meeting.

It took less than one month for the district to

- visit New Pathways and observe Lisa in her classroom;
- interview all of Lisa's teachers and most of the staff;
- interview my husband and me;
- hire four educational consultants to complete a Comprehensive Individual Assessment, which included speech-language, psychoeducational, and psychological evaluation;
- complete a Functional Analysis of Behavior by yet another consultant;
- complete a Functional Behavior Assessment and Behavior Intervention by—you guessed it—yet still another consultant.

Not only were these tests scheduled and completed in just one month, but we had the typewritten results and reports in our hands four days later—all 81 pages! Clearly, the school district was dead-set on proving that they were leaving no stone unturned in creating a plan for Lisa based on every psychological and educational test on the planet. *Amazing how quickly things moved when they were being sued.*

On the same day that we received the hefty package of reports, we also received a notice for an ARD in three days so that the committee "can review the new and updated assessment that has been conducted and develop an individualized educational program based on this information." *Again, no grass was growing under their feet. Only three days until the ARD instead of the usual two months.*

In the three days that I had to review the 81 pages of reports before the ARD convened, I tried to digest as much as I could so that I would be ready to participate fully.

There was a room full of experts present at the ARD, eighteen in all. In addition, Lisa's teacher from New Pathways joined us via conference call. Besides Bill and me, in attendance were two of the lawyers representing the school in our lawsuit, our attorney, the registrar, the chair of the English department, counselors, special education teachers, a behavior specialist, the vocational coordinator, the consultants who did the testing, and of course, the district's splendidly-dressed director of special education herself.

It was an impressive group that would have made Lisa feel very important if she had been there. They certainly wanted to prove that every possible resource was being tapped, by sheer numbers of experts if nothing else.

These school professionals had developed an Individualized Educational Plan so complex that it took three different ARD meetings to go over everything. In the end, there were over 100 pages of recommended services, educational goals, behavior objectives, behavior intervention plans, classroom management strategies, crisis management plans, health management plans, discipline procedures, graduation requirements, and vocational training proposals.

It was mind-boggling. So many people, so much time, and so many financial resources were being focused on Lisa. *Where was this effort two and a half years ago? Were they trying to intimidate us into dropping the legal proceedings?*

Chapter 44

Coming Home

On May 1, one month before the end of the school year, Lisa began the gradual transition from New Pathways to the public school. This meant that she would be transported at the public school's expense, back and forth between the public school and New Pathways. She would be picked up at New Pathways in the morning and returned in the afternoon three days the first week, then five days the second week. Then she would be discharged from New Pathways and come home to live and attend public school.

Catherine Jacobs, a behavior specialist with the school district, was assigned to Lisa on a one-on-one basis while she was at school in the SIP, or Significant Intervention Program. She would pick Lisa up at our home every morning and take her home after school. In addition, Catherine would be available 24/7 to give us support at home.

The school district was bending over backwards and making every possible effort for us. Remember, the lawsuit was still ongoing at this time. These efforts would make the district look great if the case went to trial.

The two-week transition period concluded without a hitch, and on May 15, 2000, Lisa was officially discharged from New Pathways and came home to live.

But it didn't take long for Lisa to reprise her pattern of running away from home. The first time occurred just one week after being discharged from New Pathways. She said she needed to go for a walk and would just walk around the block. She assured us she would be back soon. When she had not returned in two hours, we called Catherine, who told us that she would go out looking for Lisa.

An hour later, Catherine walked up our sidewalk with Lisa in tow. Catherine had found her several blocks away, just sitting on the street curb. Since Catherine was the behavior expert, I let her handle the discussion and set the consequences.

Three days later, I went into Lisa's room to wake her for school. She wasn't there. Then I discovered that my handbag and cell phone were missing. I really didn't know where to look for her this time because she hadn't been out of New Pathways long enough to make new friends. Catherine made a few calls to no avail.

Around 3 p.m. that same day, we received a call from Eddie, who had attended New Pathways at one point but was now living with his parents. Apparently, Lisa had called him, and he wanted to let us know she was all right. I asked him if he knew any details about what Lisa had done, and he related what she had told him.

She had run away just after midnight and called a young man named Clay, who had at one time been a resident at New Pathways, to come and get her. She spent the night at Clay's home, and Clay had taken her the next morning to the Galleria, from where she called Eddie. I suspected that she wanted to come home but didn't want to call me, so she called Eddie, knowing he would call us.

I drove to the Galleria, found her exactly where she had told Eddie she was waiting, and questioned her about what happened. She said she didn't remember anything except that she had smoked marijuana with Clay. She feared that she may have been given a date-rape drug such as GHB or Rohypnol since she couldn't remember anything that happened.

I called our family physician and spoke to his nurse. She recommended we take Lisa to the emergency room for an examination in case there had been a sexual assault. When Lisa, Bill, and I arrived at the emergency room of our local hospital, we were taken immediately into an examination room, where Lisa was given a forensic examination by a trained sexual assault examiner. During the exam a sexual assault evidence collection kit, or rape kit, was used for evidence collection, and the police were called.

After about an hour the examiner came out to where Bill and I were waiting and reported there was vaginal bruising consistent with the insertion of a foreign object, but there was no semen found. There was no way to test for presence of date-rape drug because of the length of time that had elapsed and because of her marijuana usage, which would compromise any results.

Bill and I agreed with the police and the examiner that legal action against anyone would be inappropriate, given the flimsy evidence of any sexual assault.

Lisa was treated for prevention of pregnancy and sexually transmitted diseases and then released around midnight, twenty four hours after she ran away. I was exhausted, and I suspected her bruising had been self-inflicted to shift attention from her running away.

Chapter 45

Settled

After the final ARD meeting, Mr. O'Dell, Bill, and I met to discuss legal strategy. Mr. O'Dell's position was that this was a good time to ask for a settlement amount because the school would not want to proceed to a hearing after they saw the evidence of the memo. He felt that we could get a large portion of the amount we were asking for, which would be "money in the hand."

Even if we went to trial for the full amount and won, the attorneys on the school district's retainer had deep pockets and could tie the litigation up in appeals for years. It might be six to eight years before we saw any money IF their appeal failed. Also, every appeal by the school would cost us more in Mr. O'Dell's fees.

His reasoning made sense, so Bill and I agreed to settle. Mr. O'Dell called a meeting with the other side and presented Goliath with an out-of-court settlement offer alongside a photocopy of the smoking-gun memo. I wish I could have been a fly on the wall in that room.

The Goliath attorneys called Mr. O'Dell the next day and agreed to the out-of-court settlement. The following week, we signed routine confidentiality papers agreeing not to divulge the amount of the settlement, and two weeks later, we received a check in an amount we were comfortable with. It didn't cover all of our costs, but it helped. The money fight was over after a six-month skirmish that somehow seemed much longer.

I battled within myself as to whether or not I should give part of the settlement to Lisa's dad since he had paid for part of her treatment. However, I finally reasoned that since he told me from the beginning that he did not want to participate in the lawsuit, he was not entitled to any of the money. If he had pitched in and paid even a portion of the attorney's fee, we would definitely have cut him in.

Chapter 46

Another Summer from Hell

With the regular school term finished, Lisa began summer school on June first. Under Catherine's close supervision, Lisa was taking a physical education class and working in the school office. She didn't like either one after about a week, so Catherine allowed her to help with the students in special education, as she had done when she was in intermediate school. Lisa really enjoyed working with these students, and they seemed to like and respond to her well. Getting her up and to school each morning became a lot easier.

Lisa was also proud of the fact that in the mail had come a certificate from New Pathways for her. She had been named "Miss Congeniality" of the New Pathways school program. *She is such an enigma. Miss Congeniality?*

Life at home was still a challenge, as Lisa still had frequent uncontrollable explosions of rage where she would throw objects around the room, punch the walls, or threaten to cut herself. Sometimes it took all three of us—Bill, Lisa's brother, and me—to hold her down and prevent her from doing something violent.Often Catherine would come over and talk with her, and occasionally our neighbors across the street would try to soothe her. They, too, had a troubled child and found that someone other than parents often have a better shot at getting through to a wildly emotional child.

Catherine worked with Lisa to find a job that she would enjoy in the evenings and on weekends. Given Lisa's intense love for animals, working with them in some capacity seemed logical, so she applied at a pet store in a nearby shopping mall. Two days later she was notified to come in and work a four-hour shift after school the next day.

I drove her to the mall and we agreed on a location to meet after she was finished working. Four hours later, she was at the agreed-upon spot but visibly upset. She didn't wait for me to ask what was wrong. In a loud wailing tone she began to complain that she had done nothing but clean animal cages all evening. In her words, "All I did was clean out shit for four hours, and it stunk."

"What did you think you would be doing at a pet store?" I asked gently.

She whined, "I thought I was going to be a pet counselor and take pets out of their cages to show to buyers. I thought I would be holding pets all evening."

During the entire drive home, I tried to explain to her the concept of "starting at the bottom" and encouraged her to do her job well with no complaining so that eventually she might be promoted to a pet counselor position. I wasn't sure I was getting through to her. She just couldn't get past her disappointment and anger about her unexpected responsibilities.

The next evening, I reinforced our conversation of the night before, and she seemed ready to go back to her job with a better attitude. I didn't realize at the time that her attitude was better because she had hatched a plan.

As I was getting into my car to drive to the mall to pick her up four hours later, she called.

"Mom, you don't need to come and pick me up because I'm getting a ride with someone I work with."

Warning bells rang in my head, so I responded, "No, Lisa. It's not acceptable to come home with anyone else. I'm on my way right now, so stay where you are."

When I arrived at our meeting place at the mall, she wasn't there. I had no idea where she had gone or with whom. The mall was now closed, but I banged on the back door of the pet store until the manager came out, and I asked him if he knew who might have given Lisa a ride home. He said no one working there would have offered her a ride and that Lisa had left early, saying she didn't want to work there anymore.

I drove home, hoping that she would be there by now, but objectively knowing better. She had disappeared again, and it wasn't until 2:00 a.m. that the phone rang.

It was Eddie, who sleepily relayed that Lisa had called him to come and get her. He told her that he would, but instead he called me and told me she had walked to an apartment complex where she thought she knew someone. She hung around for awhile and then got scared when she saw some guys with guns in their belts walking around.

I wanted to leave her there—natural consequences and all that—but how could I? The area had a reputation for guns and gangs, and I just couldn't leave her at night in the middle of all that. So, I brought her home.

I conferred with behavior specialist Catherine about consequences, but frankly, consequences had little to no effect on her behavior, and there was not much left that we hadn't already taken away from her. She always found ways out of the house despite the fact that we had literally turned it into a prison with locked windows and doors.

Catherine agreed with me and admitted that she was stumped, too. *Not even a trained specialist had the solution for Lisa's problems.*

I felt as if I were on a perpetual roller coaster. Some days were fine, but I was always bobbing and weaving, waiting for the next chaotic event and unable to predict it. I seemed to be revolving around her axis, and I was spinning out of orbit.

Sometime later in June, Eddie called me and asked if Lisa could attend a family barbecue the following Saturday after-noon so his family could meet her. I replied in the affirma-tive because his previous actions when Lisa had run away had always been responsible and because this was a family get-together during the day.

I drove Lisa to Eddie's uncle's home, where the barbecue was taking place, and I met his family. Eddie agreed to drive Lisa home that same evening before 11 p.m.

Eleven o'clock…eleven fifteen…eleven thirty and no sign of Lisa and Eddie. They finally called at 11:45 p.m. to say that they were on their way. An hour later, they still had not arrived. I repeatedly called Eddie's cell phone, but no one ever answered.

The next morning, Sunday, I drove to his uncle's home, but no one was there. I drove back that evening, and again no one was at home. I left a note saying Lisa had no medication with her and they needed to contact me immediately.

Finally, two days later, Eddie called. He said that Lisa was with him at his home but that she wouldn't leave. He wanted advice on how to get her to go home. *Wow! He lasted three and a half days with her! Amazing.*

I knew she wouldn't respond to me, so I suggested that he ask her to call her dad in Atlanta. Her dad advised her to go home, but she still refused.

Finally the next day, Lisa called me and asked to come back home. Eddie dropped her off around noon. She had been gone over four days, without medication the entire time. I was able to get her in to see a therapist that afternoon and made an ap-pointment with her psychiatrist for the following week.

A few days later, Lisa was upstairs in her room when we heard a chilling scream. Bill and I ran upstairs to discover leaping flames erupting from an artificial plant in her room. Bill grabbed the fire extinguisher we kept upstairs and quickly doused the flames.

Lisa was genuinely shaken and confessed that she had used a lighter to see if the leaves on the plant would burn. When the plant burst into flames, she screamed.

There was no major damage except to the plant and to her nearby backpack. However, just a few seconds more, and the bedspread and curtains would have caught fire, perhaps engulfing the entire room in flames.

She was getting totally out of hand again. Bill and I were pouring all of our emotional resources into trying to survive the reality of her mental illness. Despite the school's position that she was almost eighteen years old and shouldn't need constant care, she still definitely needed twenty-four hour supervision.

Chapter 47

'N Sync

June was still not over and already she had gotten a job, lost it, run away several times, and started a fire. Despite these escapades, Catherine was still determined to bring Lisa into the mainstream.

Catherine arranged foursome luncheons for herself, her daughter, Lisa, and me. She took Lisa on shopping trips and helped her pick out "preppy," as Lisa called them, clothes. She arranged for her daughter and her daughter's friends to meet with Lisa for coffee at Starbuck's. Catherine believed that if Lisa were exposed to the acceptable behavior of her daughter and her daughter's friends, she could emulate them.

Lisa hated every minute of it. She didn't want to be like them and called them "snooty."

I knew none of it would work. It wasn't as if Lisa had never been exposed to mainstream behavior, for goodness' sakes! My husband and I were college professors, not hillbillies from the backwoods. We had taken Lisa to musicals, the ballet, and enrolled her in modeling classes and finishing schools. She had a closet full of nice clothes. Did Catherine think Lisa had never been exposed to polite society?

Lisa's problem was that no one knew how to address her mental issues because nobody could figure out what they were.

Her psychiatrist had mentioned something called borderline personality disorder, but he said it couldn't be diagnosed until adulthood, and there was no treatment anyway. *If the mental health community and I had only known then what we know now about BPD and its successful treatment if diagnosed early.*

The only suggestion from Catherine that Lisa embraced and indeed was excited about was attending an 'N Sync concert. Lisa loved the boy band 'N Sync, so I purchased two expensive tickets near the stage where we could almost reach out and touch them.

Lisa had agreed to wear some of her "preppy" clothes and had a wonderful time. Another of her favorites, the female singer Pink, was the warm-up act, which added to her delight. I was happy because she was happy, but I had cotton in my ears the entire night. *Man, it was loud!*

The natural high from seeing and hearing her favorite boy band didn't last long, however. A few days later, Lisa became intensely depressed and experienced hallucinations with voices telling her to cut herself.

Her psychiatrist was out of town, but the doctor on call immediately admitted her to the psychiatric hospital. She was an in-patient for five days, during which time she was stabilized with medication. I visited every day and attended daily group therapy sessions with her. I was often the only parent there.

I was horrified by some of the experiences shared by the other adolescents on Lisa's unit during these group sessions. There were stories of child abuse, neglect, parental drug use, and even one boy who was forced to perform oral sex on his mortician-father's corpses.

When Lisa reluctantly agreed to speak about her "bad life experiences," I was stunned by what she said. At first, she seemed not to be able to think of anything, but finally spoke, "I just hate my life. My mom and stepdad are always dragging me to plays and ball games and things, and I don't want to go."

There was silence in the room until one girl softly spoke up, "Oh, my God. I wish I had that problem. What are you complaining about?"

I don't know if Lisa realized how ridiculous her complaint was and how lucky the others thought she was. I think she was searching to find some reason to explain and justify her emotions. She was in mental anguish because of her illness, and there just didn't seem to be any outside forces causing it. This was confusing to her. *All she knew was that she was miserable and didn't know why.*

Discharge from the psych hospital occurred on the last day of June with the anti-psychotic medication Risperdal added to her growing list of meds. We were counseled about its side effects, which include body tremors and weight gain, among about two dozen others. She returned to summer school the next day.

The month was finally over. I hoped that the tumultuous weeks in June were due to the adjustment of being at home after two and a half years in treatment centers. July certainly had to be better…didn't it?

Chapter 48

Even the Behavior Specialist Is No Match for Lisa

Despite the family cruise fiasco six months earlier, I still felt the bone-crushing need to take a happy, normal family vacation, so I convinced Bill that we should do something fun for the 4th of July holiday weekend. Our little family of four—Bill, Brian, Lisa, and I—drove to the southern Gulf Coast of Texas where we rented a condo on the beach for three nights.

It wasn't a disaster, but it was again far less than I had hoped. Lisa kept sneaking away and disappearing for hours at a time, charging phone calls to Eddie on our room's phone, and even calling the police on one occasion when she said that "some guy flashed her on the beach."

The weekend could have been worse. The new medication seemed to be stabilizing her volatile moods. *I guess, after last month, my expectations were low.*

A week later, on a Sunday evening around 11 p.m. as Lisa was presumably asleep upstairs, two police officers rang our doorbell. They stated they had received a phone call from someone named Eddie, who reported that Lisa was trying to hang herself out of grief because they had broken up.

We hurried up the stairs with the officers to find Lisa in bed but with a red mark around her neck from tying a shoestring around it. She had taken the portable phone upstairs when she went to bed and had called Eddie. They had a fight and she told him she was hanging herself.

She had perfected this "shoestring hanging" at Six Meadows and New Pathways, so she knew she could create a frightening mark on her neck with a shoestring. *Did she really want to hang herself or just make it appear so to get attention?*

Bill and I explained to the officers that Lisa was an emotionally disturbed child. They spent at least fifteen minutes talking with her in calm tones until they were satisfied that she was stabilized, and then they left.

The next day, with the marks very visible on her neck, Lisa told everyone at school that her brother had tried to choke her.

Catherine called and said Lisa had been hanging around that morning with a girl named Addison, whom she had met at our church's teen organization. Catherine didn't think Addison was a good influence and that at the moment, Catherine didn't know where they were. *Even Catherine, who gets paid to watch Lisa at all times, had lost her.*

Catherine phoned back a few minutes later, saying she had found Lisa and Addison in an empty classroom watching television and using the telephone in the room to call Eddie.

When I arrived at the school an hour before dismissal to take Lisa to her therapist appointment, Catherine met me at my car and said that Lisa was gone. We assumed she had left the school with Addison, but of course, there was no answer at Addison's home. I left a message there for someone to call me.

I continued to the therapist appointment alone. The therapist listened to my story of recent events and advised me to continue parenting Lisa as I had been doing, by using consequences and by impressing upon her how her actions affect other people.

I went home and waited for a phone call. Shortly after Bill and I finished dinner, Addison's mother called. She told me Lisa was at her home claiming to be pregnant with no place to go. Lisa had also tried to convince Addison and her mother that I was making everyone think that Lisa was mentally ill when it was really I who was.

Lisa began angrily packing her belongings as soon as she was back home and declared that she was leaving. I called Catherine, who just happened to be having dinner with two other special education teachers, so all three of them came to our home and tried to reason with Lisa. They explained all the ramifications of leaving home and going out into the dangerous world alone, but Lisa insisted on leaving.

Catherine pulled me aside and suggested that we allow Lisa to leave. She felt that Lisa would quickly change her mind and come back home.

So, we told Lisa she could leave. We all hugged and wished her good luck, and she walked out the door. Catherine and the other two ladies left, leaving Bill and me to worry alone about whether or not we had done the right thing.

About an hour later, Lisa called from a service station a half mile away, saying she wanted to come home. I told her she was welcome but that she would have to walk back. I half expected her not to come back, but about thirty minutes later, there she was at the door.

The next day she asked for permission to invite Addison to sleep over. I explained why her behavior with Addison recently had been troubling and that I did not want the responsibility of supervising both her and Addison. Lisa became angry and proclaimed that she no longer wanted to live at home and would find somewhere else to live.

She searched through the telephone book and located the number for Covenant House in the Montrose area of Houston. Covenant House is an international network that helps homeless and runaway kids stay off the streets. She called the number and told the intake supervisor that she could not live at home any longer and had no other place to go. She listened for a few moments and then hung up, declaring that Covenant House said she could stay there but that she had to find her own way there.

Eager to play out this newest sequence of events, Bill and I helped her pack and drove her to the Montrose area near downtown Houston to Covenant House.

We waited in the car while she was interviewed. I looked at the adjoining lot where there was a basketball court. No one was playing, but there was a cluster of tattered and pierced teens sitting on the curb. Many of them had do-rags or bandanas wrapped around their heads, and their arms were marked with tattoos. They must have been rejects from Covenant House and were now left to wander the streets, homeless.

We didn't wait long. Very soon, Lisa exited the building, walking slowly and deliberately toward us, as if she were calculating what to do next. Finally, she approached the car and in a tone heavy with resentment and reluctance, expressed her desire to go back home.

The intake officer had explained to her that Covenant House was an emergency shelter, not a residence for emotionally disturbed youth. She was given a list of other shelters and resources and sent on her way.

When we arrived home, Lisa didn't say much but was obviously still agitated, so Bill and I suggested that she call her dad. Her dad was able to soothe her a bit and suggested she call a couple of family friends. One was a friend of her granny's, Barbara, and the other was her former babysitter, Joan.

Both kept the conversations light and suggested that Lisa do something fun, like bake cookies, just as she used to do with her granny. After thirty minutes of conversations with these people who truly cared about her, Lisa became very compliant and even a bit penitent. She was an angel the rest of the evening.

In fact, the next two weeks were blessedly uneventful with no major problems. We kept her busy with a variety of activities, but the one she liked most was a one-week workshop sponsored by the S.P.C.A. during which she participated in fun, hands-on learning activities with animals in the shelter. I had to drive thirty miles each way in Houston traffic twice a day to get her there, but the change in her attitude made any inconvenience worth it.

She was also enjoying the social group for teenagers at our church called Life Teen. This was where she had met Addison, but she also met other teens she enjoyed spending time with.

Then school began for the fall.

Chapter 49

Senior Year

The first day of school for her senior year brought an abrupt change in our family routine, of course, and I was afraid that Lisa would have difficulty coping. I kept in touch with Catherine throughout the day, and she reported that Lisa was learning her schedule and following all the rules.

Since she had had such a successful day at school, I allowed her to meet a young man from Life Teen at Starbucks, the current teenage hangout. As Lisa had promised, she called me within an hour to pick her up. She seemed fine and happy and went upstairs to watch television around 4 p.m.

Bill had had surgery early that morning, so we were both exhausted and decided to take a nap. We were startled out of our slumber by a telephone call from Officer Elliott, who said that Lisa was in our car at the Kroger store parking lot about eight blocks away. A young man from the neighborhood had seen her and had alerted the officer to the fact that she had no license and didn't know how to drive.

I bounced out of bed and drove to the Kroger store in our other vehicle. As I was driving her home from Kroger, Lisa became angry and threatened to jump out of the moving vehicle. When I stopped at a stop sign, she threw the door open and leaped out of the car. She ran down the street and disappeared around the corner. I had no choice but to go home. I arranged for someone to pick up our other car that was still in the Kroger parking lot and waited for Lisa to return.

When she returned home an hour or so later, she took a steak knife from the kitchen and ran upstairs with it. She threatened to use it on herself, saying that she wanted to die.

I bounded upstairs to her room, and her agitation escalated as I wrestled her for the knife. I managed to get it away from her, but as I did, she pulled away and ran back down the stairs into the kitchen.

She pulled a pointed, serrated carving knife out of a kitchen drawer and threatened to use it on herself. She began shredding her tee shirt to show me she was serious. As I lunged toward her, she raised the knife and warned me to come no closer. She was clearly in the midst of another meltdown.

I backed away from her and turned toward the telephone on the kitchen cabinet to call for help. At that point, she threw the knife at me. It caught me in the flesh of my calf, causing a deep gash that began bleeding profusely.

She then went to the kitchen cabinet and began smashing drinking glasses on the floor. After the fourth glass, I managed to physically restrain her. I called Catherine, who arrived within minutes.

Lisa gradually became more composed but refused to talk to Catherine for about twenty minutes, after which she began relating her fears about school. She said that she had been spending lunchtime with Addison and some of her friends, who had provided her with cigarettes. After a long discussion with Catherine about how to distance herself from them and use other coping mechanisms for her anxiety, she went to bed.

While the two of them were talking, Bill helped me bandage my leg. He wanted to take me to the emergency room, but I didn't want to leave Lisa. Plus, I was emotionally drained. I felt as if my body were just a shell with nothing inside. The stress of these confrontations with Lisa was taking a toll on me, and the worst part was not knowing how to help her. *No, the worst part was my acute and intense fear that she would never get better.*

My husband's support, patience, and understanding were all that stood between myself and a nervous breakdown. My hair began to fall out, I couldn't sleep, and I had difficulty concentrating on anything. It was taking all of my strength and focus to teach my classes, which left me depleted and exhausted at the end of the day. In addition to my maternal anxieties about Lisa, I was entering menopause, with all of its annoying symptoms.

I began seeing a psychiatrist, who prescribed an anti-depressant and anti-anxiety medication. Now, instead of not being able to sleep at all, I wanted to sleep all the time.

Lisa's psychiatrist doubled her anti-psychotic medication after the knife incident, but two days later, we received a call early afternoon from one of Lisa's teachers, saying that Lisa had left campus.

She had gone to the nurse's office for her medication around 11 a.m. and had not returned. *This is exactly why we had sued the school district! Their 89 pages of education plans weren't worth the paper they were written on if they couldn't even keep her in the classroom. Where was Lisa's one-on-one behavior specialist when she bolted?*

At around 4:30 p.m. Lisa sauntered into the house and said that she had been walking around the apartments near the school and then had gone to Starbucks to wait for the other students to get out of school. She said that she hated school and wanted to quit, find a job, and live on her own or else go back to Creek Ranch School in New Mexico.

I called Catherine, who came over with two other teachers, and we talked to Lisa about the ramifications of dropping out of school, such as working for minimum wage, not having enough money for a car, etc.

After about twenty minutes, Lisa informed us she had had enough of the discussion, went upstairs, packed her backpack, and proceeded to walk out the door. We didn't try to stop her; in fact, Catherine and I reminded her to bring her medication along this time.

At Catherine's suggestion I called around to the people I thought she might go to and asked them not to take her in, regardless of what sob story she told them.

Bill and I received no word from her until about 9 p.m. when she called from a bowling alley.

"Hi, Mom. I just wanted to tell you I'm okay. I'm with Lynn."

"Who is Lynn?" I wanted to keep the conversation going.

"Lynn lived here when we were in seventh grade. Then they moved away, and now they're back. Is Dad still coming into town tomorrow?"

Her dad was coming to Houston from Atlanta the next day to spend some time with friends and family, so I asked, "How are you going to see your dad if you're not at home? You haven't seen him in a long time."

"I might come home tomorrow since Dad is coming. But I'm not coming until after school is out so you can't make me go to school. Gotta go. Bye."

About two hours later she called again, saying she would come home around midnight that night but that she would not go to school the next day.

I told her that was unacceptable, that she was welcome to come back home but that she would have to obey the house rules, which included going to school.

She didn't come home until the next day around 5 p.m. She refused to talk except to say that the only reason she came home was because her dad had come into town to spend the weekend with her. She stomped up the stairs and into her room, slamming the door shut.

203

She didn't re-appear until the next morning when her dad arrived at the door. *I breathed a huge sigh of relief when her dad drove off with her. I felt as if I had been holding my breath for days.*

It was Saturday, and I was using the day to prepare my lessons for the new semester at Houston Community College which would begin the following Monday. Lisa was still with her dad.

Around noon the doorbell rang. I answered it and found two young ladies about Lisa's age and another woman who looked to be about 25 years old. They wanted to speak to me.

They introduced themselves as Lynn, Heather, and Gail. Lynn was the girl Lisa knew from seventh grade with whom she told me she had stayed the previous week. As it turned out, Lynn's mother would not let Lisa spend the night with them, so Heather, another friend from middle school, took Lisa to Gail's home. Gail was Heather's sister, and Heather lived with Gail, Gail's husband and their two children.

Lisa gave Gail and her family an award-winning sob story. She told them she had been raped by her stepfather, had his baby, lived on the streets, and hadn't eaten in days. Feeling sorry for her, Gail let her stay.

The three had come to my home to inform me that Lisa had been a bad houseguest. They asserted that Lisa had been "coming on" to Gail's husband, as well as to Heather's boyfriend and to the lawn maintenance man/ gardener. Furthermore, Gail's car was stolen sometime over the weekend, and they suspected Lisa to be in some way involved because she was one of only a few people who knew how to start it.

I just sat there in silence, not knowing what to say. I finally apologized to them for their trouble and explained that nothing Lisa had told them was true. When they left, I collapsed into Bill's strong arms and cried.

The next evening, Lisa's dad, David, brought her back home. It was about eight o'clock in the evening, so I suggested that she take a shower and get ready for bed because the next day was a school day. She responded by announcing to her father and me that she was not going back to school.

David and I reinforced each other by declaring in no uncertain terms that the topic of school was not up for discussion. This started an escalating rage, which included Lisa threatening to stab herself with a table knife and then smashing a glass on the floor, all the while shrieking that she was not going to return to school.

Her dad and I called Catherine, who spoke with Lisa on the phone for a few minutes before agreeing to let Lisa have one more day with her dad since he had come all the way from Georgia to see her. In return, Lisa had to promise to return to school on Tuesday and also promise to talk with her dad about her feelings during their time together. Lisa agreed, went upstairs, showered, and was asleep by 9 p.m.

I was not in favor of this "deal" they had struck, but Catherine was the expert. I was no behavior expert, but even I could see that Lisa would agree to anything that benefitted her in the short run. She had no intention of fulfilling her end of the bargain.

David picked her up around 8:30 a.m. Monday morning. Their plan was to have breakfast and then go to the mall. However, by noon they had already returned. David said she began screaming uncontrollably in the mall when they talked about going to school the next day.

We called behavior expert Catherine, who met with David and Lisa in the afternoon and convinced Lisa to go to school the next day if her father went with her on the bus and stayed with her all day. *Again with the deals and the promises.*

The next morning, David rode with Lisa on the bus to school. Around 11 a.m., Lisa began acting out, pulling her hair and screaming. She said she felt like killing herself and others.

Catherine was called in, but she was not able to quiet Lisa, and Lisa bolted from school. David took off to find her and after about a half hour, he spotted her walking toward home.

I had been in class and not aware of any of the commotion until I arrived home. After hearing the story from David, I called her psychiatrist, who told me to take her to the psychiatric hospital and admit her to the adolescent unit.

David went back to Atlanta. *Lucky him.*

L isa slept most of the first two days in the hospital and missed all of her groups, so her doctor locked her out of her room during the day. In response, she began pulling her hair out and self-abusing with her eating utensils and anything else she could find. She remained on suicide watch and had to eat her meals with her fingers in her room.

As her eighteenth birthday approached, her doctor said he would release her on her birthday if she had 48 hours of good behavior; otherwise, she would have to go to the adult intensive care unit. She managed to control her actions and was released on her eighteenth birthday, September first, with a prescribed increase in her Depakote dosage.

As we arrived home from the hospital and got out of the car, Lisa demanded five dollars from me and said she wanted to go to Starbucks. I refused because I knew she just wanted to buy cigarettes with it. She then flew into one of her rages and grabbed the hedge clippers that were nearby. She swung as hard as she could and smashed the windshield of Bill's car.

She bolted out of the garage and down the street on foot. The violence frightened me, so I locked all the doors of our home and called the police. In about five minutes, I heard her pounding on the patio door, trying to get in. She became further agitated as she heard me on the phone canceling her family birthday celebration for that evening.

She ran around the house to the front door, picked up a cement garden decoration, and raised it as if to hurl it through the stained glass of the front door. Bill quickly opened the door and restrained her before she could throw the five-pound block of concrete.

I allowed her to come inside, but again Bill had to physically restrain her as she kicked and physically lashed out at us. A police officer arrived just as Lisa threw a punch at Bill, but he blocked it and continued to hold her down.

Another officer then arrived, followed by about thirty minutes of "talking her down." We filed a police report but did not press any charges. By the time the officers left, she was calm and rational and compliant.

I guess her psychiatrist would say it was a typical borderline episode. It was not a very good eighteenth birthday for her. Or for us. I didn't know how much more of this emotional trauma I could take. I needed to find more strength, so I began attending a weekly prayer novena at my church, asking for strength, guidance, and wisdom.

Chapter 50

Eighteen and Out

Bill and I locked our bedroom door at night because we feared for our safety. We also kept our wallets, money, and keys locked up; otherwise, Lisa would steal the money and our car and run away. *This was no way to live.*

My therapist agreed. She explained that we have a right to protect, defend, and take care of ourselves and that I needed to set definite limits, or boundaries, regarding the behaviors of Lisa that we would not accept. She went on to say that since Lisa was now legally an adult, she had to comply with our rules or find somewhere else to live.

She advised that we set the boundary clearly, preferably without anger, and in as few words as possible. We should not justify, apologize for, or rationalize the limit we were setting, nor should we argue. "Just set the boundary calmly, firmly, and re-spectfully," she added.

Despite all of our efforts to keep all money hidden, Lisa still managed to find fifteen dollars to steal while we were asleep. Bill and I sat down with her and in a calm voice, I held her hands, looked her in the eyes and said, "Lisa, you have stolen from us.If you steal from us again, you cannot live with us anymore." I asked if she understood, and she nodded.

She stole again five days later, and we kept our promise. *She was out.*

I hadn't really planned what to do if—when—I would have to carry out my ultimatum. Although she was eighteen, she was as mature as a twelve-year-old and I just couldn't turn her out into the street. We had exhausted the list of shelters that Covenant House had given us. There was no place else that she could go except back to New Pathways.

During every phone call during her first week back at New Pathways, Lisa insisted that she didn't want to be there. According to her, she didn't want to be told what to do all the time, and she didn't need to be there. She said she needed to be on her own and not babied. She insisted on checking herself out, which she could legally do, now that she was eighteen.

Her therapist, her doctor, the New Pathways psychologist, and I all tried to talk her out of leaving. I conferred with her doctors by phone, and the consensus was that if she wanted to go, we had to let her go. She was legally an adult now.

The psychologist called Lisa into her office and informed her that she could leave if that was still what she wanted. She then suggested that Lisa had better start making phone calls to find a shelter or some other place to go.

The next day, around 3 p.m., New Pathways staff drove her into Houston and dropped her off at Magnificat House, a women's shelter, from where she called me to say she was getting checked in.

I was crushed and could hardly speak through my tears, but I continued to hope that perhaps Magnificat House would have a program or counseling and some sort of housing for her.

The next morning, Lisa and a friend named Dina showed up at our doorstep around 11 a.m. She informed me that she had given away to New Pathways residents many of her belongings, including several pairs of shoes, clothes, an expensive radio, and CDs, and she needed to get some things from her room upstairs.

She explained that she had met Dina at Magnificat House and that the staff there had given her bus tokens to come home and pick up her belongings.

I helped her pick out a few clothes and some toiletries, put them in a bag, and gave her bus fare to return to Magnificat House.

I hadn't heard from her for two days, when she called.

"Hi, Mom."

"Lisa! Where are you? Are you okay?"

"Yes, I'm fine, but I got stung by a bee and had to go to the emergency room for a shot because I started to swell up. But I'm fine now."

"How do you like Magnificat House?"

"It's okay, but they told me I have to go somewhere else because I'm not stable enough, so they gave me a list of places I could stay."

"Where are you going to go?"

"I'm not going to any of them. I'm going to stay with my boyfriend."

"What boyfriend?" I asked in disbelief.

"I met him on the streets near Covenant House."

At this point I was certain that she had not been staying at Magnificat House because they wouldn't just let her loiter on the streets. They had very strict rules.

I told her that I knew she hadn't been staying at Magnificat House and that I was worried about her and where she was living.

She surprised me with her subdued response, "Mom, it's really hard being out and staying alive."

My heart skipped a beat. Perhaps in her moment of weakness I could persuade her to return to New Pathways! Unfortunately, she quickly recovered and replied in a more chipper tone, "But I'm enjoying myself."

She continued to call me about every other day from pay phones. Sometimes the calls were collect, but other times she called using coins. When I asked where she was getting the money to call and to eat, she responded that she "spanges" on street corners.

This word "spange" was a new one for me, and I was taken aback. When I asked her what that meant, she explained that it meant to beg or panhandle. Apparently, it is a shortening of the phrase, "spare changing."

Well, this was a new low. My own daughter was a street person, standing on corners begging for money. I wanted to rescue her with every cell in my body, but she didn't want to be rescued. My therapist encouraged me to be strong and to let go. She gave me a phrase that I repeated to myself often, "Let go and let God."

She assured me that it was really good that Lisa continued to keep in touch with me. That meant she had strong ties to me and some empathy for my concern for her.

My therapist continued, "It's possible that Lisa is trying to live the rebellious teenaged years that she had never experienced while she was in residential treatment centers. Not only that, but she hasn't yet hit bottom. Since she continues to call you periodically, you will know when she hits bottom. Then she will be ready to live a more normal life."

Normal? I'd given up on normal, whatever that was. I would settle for living without a gnawing in the pit of my stomach.

A few days later, I received in the mail Lisa's discharge summary from New Pathways. Her diagnoses upon leaving, at legal-adult-age of eighteen were

Axis I: attention deficit hyperactivity disorder, impulse control disorder, oppositional defiant disorder

Axis II: borderline personality disorder. *There it was—now that she was eighteen, they were willing to call it what it was.*

Axis III: cerebral dysrhythmia, nocturnal enuresis

Axis IV: educational, social, and primary support group problems

Axis V: GAF level at discharge 45.

The most significant difference from her Six Meadows discharge summary a year ago was the removal of pervasive developmental disorder and replacement with borderline personality disorder. The other diagnoses remained virtually the same. Even her GAF functioning level was the same.

Her discharge medications were Depakote, Zoloft, Clomipramine, birth control pills, Risperdal, and methylphenidate, for which they gave her prescriptions.

Chapter 51

The Streets

I notified the school district that Lisa would not be returning to classes. Their response was to schedule yet another ARD.

I did not attend. I saw no reason to attend. Plus, I was afraid of what I might say because I was angry. In my opinion, they had totally botched everything despite all the experts and Ph.D.s and vows to create a successful program for her. *She is living on the streets. Do they consider that successful? Besides, she was eighteen now and legally in charge of her own education.*

Soon after the scheduled ARD meeting, a thick manila envelope addressed to Lisa came in the mail. Inside were about thirty pages of documents. The cover letter stated:

"Dear Lisa,

On 9/15/00, the Admission, Review, and Dismissal Committee met to discuss special education planning and services for you. The ARD Committee recommended placement at SIP (Significant Intervention Program). Your mother has informed us that you would not be returning to school; however, we want you to be fully aware of the ARD Committee's plan, and we want you also to know that it is in place should you return." *Well, here we were—full circle. The best they could come up with was the same program that didn't work in the first place, three years ago.*

The next time Lisa phoned, I read the cover letter to her. Her response was, "I'm not going back there."

She hung up and went back to her peripatetic life on the streets. All I could do was wait until she called again.

The next call from Lisa came about a week later. She left a telephone message mid-afternoon, saying she had called an ambulance to take her to the trauma center of Ben Taub Hospital, part of Houston's community-owned hospital system, because she was having seizures.

That evening, Dr. Eve Taylor, a psychiatrist at Ben Taub, called for background info to help her decide whether to admit Lisa or not. She must have decided against it because Lisa called at 3 a.m. and asked me to come and get her.

I refused and told her to use the resources at the hospital to find a place to go. *She couldn't have it both ways, independent yet wanting to be rescued when times got tough.*

I got three collect calls from her the next day as she waited at the hospital for someone from Harris County Psychiatric Center (HCPC), part of the University of Texas Health System, to arrive. I was becoming somewhat irked by the third costly call, so I abruptly informed her that, although I was happy to hear from her because I wanted to know that she was all right, the calls were becoming excessive and costly.

She responded sharply, "Well, what do you want me to do? Kill myself?"

In as composed a voice as I could muster, I told her, "No, I just want you to get yourself out of the jam you have gotten yourself into."

"Well, I can't go back to Montrose because "they are all mad at me."

"Who is mad at you?" I demanded.

"Everybody on the streets. Never mind. I'll just wait for HCPC." And she hung up.

The Montrose area of downtown Houston partly consisted of a bohemian counterculture of gays, lesbians, and street people, especially around the six-block area surrounding the intersection of Montrose Avenue and Westheimer Boulevard, near Covenant House.

The street people are said to have an unwritten code or set of rules that govern interaction among street people. It seems that Lisa must have violated this code in some way, since she felt she couldn't go back there.

I didn't hear from her at all during the night, but late the next morning, she called from the Harris County Psychiatric Center, having been admitted. I immediately drove downtown to see her, but she had been given strong psychiatric medications and was sleepily incoherent.

I returned the next day, after teaching my classes, carrying with me a shirt, shoes, and shorts for Lisa. She had told me that the only clothing she had was what she was wearing. Everything else had been stolen on the streets.

Two days later, while I was teaching, Lisa called our home number in the morning and again in the afternoon, leaving messages saying she was going to a YMCA shelter because the limit of stay at HCPC was three days.

That evening, just as we were sitting down to dinner, a police officer called to say that Lisa had asked him to call me to inform me that she was on her way from the YMCA to Ben Taub Hospital in an ambulance because she had been sexually assaulted.

About two hours later a nurse called to say the story Lisa had told at the trauma center to the policeman investigating her claim did not make any sense and that when she was pressed for more information, she suddenly left the hospital, and they didn't know where she had gone.

I thanked the nurse for the information and fell into my husband's arms, sobbing, "How do I let go?" He reminded me that I *had* to find the strength to let go. *I had to let go and let God.*

That night at 3 a.m., Lisa called from a Walgreen's store, saying that she and a friend she had met on the streets named Jennifer were going to live with someone named Mark in Livingston, Texas. She even gave me Mark's telephone number if I needed to reach her.

I didn't hear from her at all for a week. Between classes I would call home to check for messages on the answering machine. The caller ID on our phone indicated that we had received a call from a pay phone one afternoon, but no message was left.

During the next two weeks, she called several times, but the charges were not being reversed anymore; they were from someone's residential phone. I made careful note of telephone numbers from the caller ID.

During one call, she said she was sick and coughing up blood and had gone to a doctor. She claimed the doctor told her she might have tuberculosis and should rest.

"Where are you now? Are you taking your psych meds?" I asked her.

"No. I don't have any more, and I'm staying with some people in Coldspring." This is a tiny town in East Texas.

"Tell me where you are, and I can meet you this weekend and bring your medications," I begged. She said she would think about it.

The next night, around 9 p.m., she called from a gas station in a small town about an hour north of Houston, complaining that she had been thrown out of the house in Coldspring when they discovered she was sick.

"I want to come home," she wailed.

We had a terrible telephone connection, and at that point, before I could reply, we lost our connection. I tried to call the number on my caller ID, but to no avail. The next time we heard from her, about two hours later, she said she was in Houston, having gotten a ride from someone who had stopped for gas at the station.

She related that the man giving her a ride wanted to know where to drop her off, so she put him on the phone, and I gave him directions to the MHMRA crisis center on Caroline Street. Unfortunately, I didn't know that the MHMRA crisis center had closed several months prior. So, of course, it wasn't long before I received another call from her, collect, and she was frantic.

"Mom! He just dumped me off in the middle of Houston, and I'm scared."

By now it was the middle of the night, but Bill and I drove into the city, picked her up at the intersection of Caroline and Alabama Streets, and transported her to the Neuropsychiatric Center at Ben Taub Hospital. The Neuropsych Center was a brand-new facility that had recently opened and was replacing the now-shuttered MHMRA crisis center. I left her with some clothes, her medications, some toiletries, and $5.

She still hasn't hit bottom—her bottom, not mine. She still calls to be rescued, and I keep rescuing her. But I can't just abandon her.

Chapter 52

Sally's House

The next day I phoned Lisa's case worker at the Neuropsych Center, who said she had given Lisa a list of personal care homes, including Magnificat House and the Salvation Army's Sally's House. The next time Lisa called, I asked her about checking them out.

She responded, "I did. They are all full except for Sally's House."

"I'll help you get settled if you want to go to Sally's House," I replied hopefully. "In fact, if you agree to Sally's House, you can come home for a night or two while we gather together some clothes and things. Then you can go to Sally's House."

She agreed, so I drove downtown to the Texas Medical Center, picked her up, and brought her home. She spent a full day and night with us, as we busied ourselves by assembling the items she would need such as a few clothes and toiletries. The next day, I drove her to Sally's House in downtown Houston.

Sally's House, part of the Salvation Army, is a transitional shelter for single women in a humble two-story building acrossfrom the enormous Minute Maid Baseball Park. The familiar red Salvation Army shield with the simple message "Doing the Most Good" was the only suggestion that this was no ordinary house. During an average six-month stay, residents must work or attend school and participate in support services designed to restore mental and physical health, upgrade professional skills, and encourage independent living.

We were both upbeat, as I helped Lisa register and went over the house rules with her. As we discussed them, my optimistic expectations began to wane. There were a lot of rules...a lot of rules. This was not a motel. It was supervised living, and I knew how Lisa was with rules and supervision.

Morning wake-up was at 6:30 and curfew was 9 p.m., after which the doors were locked. The bedroom area had to be kept clean, and there was only one telephone and one television in the house. These were supervised by staff. Residents also were required either to work or go to school. Since she had not yet officially finished high school, Lisa had to attend a GED program.

My stomach was sinking. I couldn't see how this was going to work, but I still had hope. It was all I had. If I lost hope, I would become like the other mothers of troubled children I had met, who had given up on their children and severed all ties to them.

As I left, I hugged Lisa, and she promised to call during allowed hours. *Oh, how I wanted Sally's House to be the answer. She would be supervised, go to school, and learn responsible independence.*

She lasted eight days at Sally's House. On the eighth night, when she didn't call, I phoned Sally's House. The house manager informed me that Lisa did not want to conform to the rules and did not want to work or go to school; therefore, she had left. Once again, I had no idea where she was.

The next day Bill and I taught our classes as usual. In the afternoon I arrived home before he did and saw that the back yard gate was open. This made me slightly uneasy, but I just assumed the electric company's meter reader had forgotten to close it.

When I opened the door to the house, I realized that a window in the family room had been smashed. I was frightened that the intruders might still be in the house, so I ran across the street and asked my neighbor for advice. A big, strapping man, he offered to check it out for me.

He searched through the house but found no one. Assuming it was safe to go inside, I called the police. They suggested I document the items that were missing and gave me a case number.

After a thorough search, I found that the places where we had in the past kept some extra cash had been shuffled through. A portable CD player and some music CDs were missing. At that point, a chill ran down my spine as I realized the intruder must have been Lisa or someone with her.

Bill came home soon after, and he agreed that Lisa indeed must have been the culprit. We were both demoralized.

Of course, Lisa denied having anything to do with the break-in when she called the next day, but deep inside I knew better.

We installed a security system the next week.

Chapter 53

Thumper's Street Family

My daughter didn't want to come home, and she didn't want to work any kind of program like the ones at Sally's House or Magnificat House, so the streets of Montrose became her home.

According to City of Houston statistics for the year 2000, about 1,500 homeless kids between the ages of 14 and 22, equally divided among males and females, were living on the streets of America's fourth-largest city. Many of them were runaways from parental neglect or abuse, while others were throwaways, meaning they had parents who had told them to leave—kicked them out.

They wander the streets, particularly around Montrose, for a substantial portion of their days and nights. In fact, Covenant House chose their location in Montrose to be near these kids.

Unfortunately, prostitution, shoplifting, drugs, and "survival sex" are all part of street life, which the kids survive the best they can. Even the young people who have a desire to get away from the street scene often find themselves economically trapped.

I was shocked to discover that, among these troubled youth, there are young women attempting to raise children in the vicious street environment. Often, these are young women who were kicked out by their parents for having a baby out of wedlock. Lacking money, these mothers frequently turn to other street kids as babysitters, thus exposing their children to immoral, unhealthy environments.

These youth live in "families" of as many as twenty adolescents, staying under bridges, squatting in deserted buildings or spangeing for enough money to spend the night crammed into a cheap motel room. They eat thrown-out food from the nearby Pizza Hut, KFC, and Wendy's. They avoid using their real names and assume "street names," often because they fear being sent home or placed in foster care.

Lisa chose "Thumper" for her street name, as in the fictional rabbit character in Disney's *Bambi*. When she told me this, I couldn't help but smile. Not only was it an innocent-sounding name as opposed to other street names like Satan and Rebel, but she chose it because of a lesson Bill had tried to teach her when she was younger. Whenever she would say something unkind or derogatory, Bill would remind her, "Do you remember what Thumper's father said?"

She would laugh and respond, "Yes, I remember. If you can't say anything nice, then don't say anything at all." It was a little game they played.

L isa stayed in touch with us, calling every other day or so just to say she was alive. Sometimes we arranged a meeting place, usually at the McDonald's parking lot, and I brought her toiletries, food, or small amounts of money.

These meetings were heart-wrenching for me. It was difficult to see her in that environment, but she seemed happy. She was always upbeat and never wanted to visit long. After a few minutes, she would tell me that I could leave. I couldn't tell if she was on drugs; she didn't act as if she were, *but then, what did I know?* I didn't ask her, partly because I didn't want to know and partly because she wouldn't have told me the truth, anyway.

She wasn't taking any of her psychiatric medications and didn't want me to provide any. She said they would just get stolen.

Several street friends usually accompanied Lisa, and I got to know them by their street names: Stormy, Dough Boy, Tennessee, Squirrel, etc. I asked Stormy, who was from California, why she was on the streets. "I don't want to be on the streets," she replied, "but it is better than being beaten up by parents who don't care."

Another street friend, Nickel, was currently enrolled in Covenant House's GED program and kept a locker there. He complained, "I don't stay at Covenant House because they don't let me wear my nail polish," which he proudly displayed. He went on, "They have too-strict rules there, like I had at home in Corpus Christi."

On one occasion, one of the young men noticed that one of my rear tires was flat. He and a friend offered to change it for me, and when they were finished, I tried to pay them. I was stunned when they refused to accept any money. One said, "We wanted to do it for Thumper's mom."

I insisted upon buying hamburgers for all of them, however, which they accepted.

Lisa had been on birth control pills while at New Pathways, but I knew she couldn't be counted upon to take them as prescribed, so one day I picked her up from Montrose and drove to Planned Parenthood. She received a complete physical exam, a three-month contraceptive injection, and a handful of free condoms, along with a long conversation about safe sex on the streets.

I have been very grateful for Planned Parenthood. Their counseling and intervention may have prevented her from an unwanted pregnancy or worse, contracting HIV.

After about six weeks on the street, Lisa grew "tired of the street scene," she told me on the phone one night, "so I'm at the Greyhound bus station with Splash. He's going to get some money from his dad, and we're going to New Orleans."

"Who is Splash, and why are you going to New Orleans?" I said, my voice rising with concern.

"He's a guy I know from Montrose."

I panicked, as usual. *New Orleans? The Houston streets were bad enough, but New Orleans?* She assured me she would be fine because Splash was a good guy. *It was small consolation.*

Three days later, she called again, still at the bus station downtown.

"Where are you?" I asked.

"We're still in Houston. We've been sleeping at the bus station for three nights now, waiting for Splash's father. I don't think he's going to come, so I'm going to leave with a guy named James. He has money, so he bought me a ticket, and we're going to New Orleans first and then to Las Vegas."

Oh, my gosh! One sin city instead of another.

At this point, she seemed to be able to take care of herself quite nicely, or at least find guys who were willing to take care of her, so I "let go" and simply asked her to call me whenever she could, trying to remember that she was chronologically an adult and there was little I could do anymore. *Except worry.*

Author's Note

Twenty years ago, borderline personality disorder was considered untreatable and hopeless. Today it is treatable and there is real hope. There is still no cure, but you can get much better. Recent research based on long-term studies of people with BPD suggest that the overwhelming majority of people will experience significant symptom remission in their lifetimes and be able to lead meaningful and productive lives with the help of treatment—either medication or psychotherapy or both.

Finding and affording treatment for BPD is a challenge, however. BPD is still very stigmatized, even in the mental health field, because of its resistance to treatment. Many therapists still don't understand the disorder, and treatment is very costly, anywhere between $80 to $150 per hour. DBT, or dialectical behavior therapy, is the preferred therapeutic intervention, and it takes years of weekly sessions to see success. Only a few insurance companies will cover the cost of DBT treatment.

Diagnosing BPD correctly in children is difficult because of its wide-ranging symptoms. Initially called "problem children," the diagnosis may first be ADHD, then perhaps bi-polar disorder. When the treatment/medication for those doesn't work, parents feel helpless until, eventually, a diagnosis of BPD may be made. Meanwhile, valuable time is lost.

It can also be complicated to get a BPD diagnosis in teens because adolescent emotional disruptions are, by nature, normal. As it was once explained to me, it is a question of degree: slamming doors when teens are mad is normal; punching walls until they break bones in their hands or cutting themselves could signify BPD. If it remains undiagnosed, families cannot find effective treatment.

Early treatment is vital. BPD does not solidify if it is treated early, and proper treatment can actually change the brain chemistry in adolescents and children. Studies have shown that adolescents adapt coping skills better and are more responsive to treatment than adults, are easier to change, and have parents around to help them cope. An early diagnosis can put a person on a path to eliminate the painful emotions and feelings of BPD.

The sooner you know, the more years of grief you can avoid.

Website: GrowingUpBorderline.com

Email: LindaBurch@GrowingUpBorderline.com

Coming in 2014...

Read on for a sneak peek at <u>Living Borderline</u> by Linda Burch, which continues Lisa's story into BPD adulthood as she battles life on the streets, drug abuse, legal problems, and stormy relationships.

Available on Kindle, in paperback at Amazon.com, & the website http://GrowingUpBorderline.com.

Living Borderline (Sneak Peek)

L isa had a new live-in boyfriend, her first since Eric moved out. John didn't have a job or a place to live, so whether he truly cared for her or not, shacking up with Lisa was a good thing with free room and board that we provided. It actually was a win-win situation for us, too, because he kept the would-be squatters out of the house. We no longer received violation letters from the townhome association for "too many people staying at the unit."

Another perk was that John guarded and dispensed Lisa's medication. He kept it in a locked box and made sure she took it as prescribed. Unfortunately, if she took her meds as prescribed, she did a lot of sleeping. John complained she was always asleep, and finally after about six months, he left, too. *Abandoned again— here we go. I waited for another suicide attempt.*

Although nearly all borderlines try at some point to escape their intense emotional pain with suicide attempts, most attempts are never fulfilled. However, ten per cent of those who attempt suicide complete it, whether by determination or by accident, for example, when help does not arrive as soon as they anticipated.

It was this ten per cent I always worried about. Something could go wrong: she might not reach me, or I might not arrive in time, or she would get too drowsy from an overdose to call 911, or the slash on her wrists would be too deep.

This time my daughter's call was a little different. She had sold her television set to buy enough crack to kill herself, she said. I winced and squeezed my eyes shut. *Oh no, here we go again.* When I arrived at her place, Lisa was already suffering the "crash" stage—exhausted, depressed, and agitated. She admitted that she had smoked the crack several hours before and thus was not in any immediate danger of dying. However, she must have bought a lot of crack because she still owed the dealer $50 in addition to the television she had already given him. She begged me to give her the money or he would "beat me up or kill me," she sobbed, "because he lives in this townhome complex."

What should I do? I can't give her the money because she may go out and buy more drugs with it. Will I be enabling her if I bail her out of the jam? Probably. But I've got to do it. Is she telling the truth about this dealer being dangerous?

I decided to pay off her debt to the drug dealer, but I refused to give her the money to do it. I thought she might use it to buy more drugs. I told her I would give it to the dealer myself. *Oh, my gosh, what was I thinking?*

Lisa resisted, but I insisted, so she called the guy and said we would meet him in the parking lot of the townhome complex. I made Lisa stay inside and watch for him from her upstairs bedroom window while I waited in my car in the parking lot. Always thinking ahead, I wanted her observing from inside in case something went wrong and police had to be called. *Right...if I were really thinking, I wouldn't be doing this.*

I didn't know what to expect. Would he be on foot? Would he be armed? Would he be drugged out? Pictures of all the drug dealers I had seen on TV raced through my mind like a video on fast-forward. Pretty soon my cell phone rang.

"Mom, he's coming through the entrance gate. He's in a silver Cadillac Escalade."

Cadillac Escalade? That's a $75,000 vehicle! I guess the illegal drug business is pretty profitable.

He pulled up next to me in my twelve-year-old Chevrolet Blazer and stayed inside his vehicle, engine running. He rolled down the passenger window, which was next to my driver side window, which I rolled down. He was dressed in stylish clothes and had a diamond earring in his ear.

I spoke first. "I understand Lisa owes you money."

He nodded, but he didn't say anything.

"Is it $50?"

Another nod.

I opened my car door and reached into his open window with the $50 in my hand. He took it without saying a word.

My mind was screaming, "Tell him to stay away from your daughter. Tell him that if he ever sells her drugs again, you will call the cops because you have his license plate number. Tell him..."

But I was too scared. I just wanted him to take the $50 and leave. Which he did.

I realized I was trembling as I took down his plate number and got out of the car. On legs that felt like rubber, I walked to the end of the street to see where he would park his Escalade and which townhome he would enter. *I don't know why. Did I think I was going to turn him into the cops? Then what? There was no evidence, and if he found out, Lisa or I could be in danger. Too many cop shows on TV.*

On my way home, I called Carol, Lisa's therapist, and related what happened. I was so upset that Lisa had turned to drugs and was afraid she was going to become dependent on them. Borderlines are at unusually high risk of drug or alcohol abuse because of their emotional instability and impulsive behavior.

They use drugs to self-medicate their pain of abandonment fears and other emotional issues they cannot deal with.

"Do I need to put her into drug rehab?" I asked Carol.

"No, this is just one of her borderline episodes. Bring her in tomorrow, and she and I will talk."

When I arrived home, my husband put his arm around me, and I buried my face in his shoulder and sobbed.

Special Acknowledgements

Sincere thanks to my dear friends
Charlotte Sodolak, Colette Schultz,
Mary Hancock, and Jeanne Huiras,
who all helped in so many ways,
from moral support to formatting.

About the Author

Linda Kana Burch is a retired college English professor who has degrees from The University of Texas at Austin and the University of Houston – Clear Lake. She lives in Houston, Texas, with her husband, Bill, and is the mother of two children, one with borderline personality disorder. She and her husband are trained instructors of the Family Connections course that was created by the National Education Alliance for Borderline Personality Disorder, and they facilitate a support group for family members of borderlines. She is also the author of *Living Borderline*, the sequel to *Growing up Borderline*, which will be published in 2014.

www.ingramcontent.com/pod-product-compliance
Lightning Source LLC
Chambersburg PA
CBHW072123270326
41931CB00010B/1653